Integral Justice

Integral Justice

Changing People Changing Structures

John J. Walsh, M.M.

ORBIS BOOKS

Maryknoll, New York 10545

Fourth Printing, August 1998

The Catholic Foreign Mission Society of America (Maryknoll) recruits and trains people for overseas missionary service. Through Orbis Books, Maryknoll aims to foster the international dialogue that is essential to mission. The books published, however, reflect the opinions of their authors and are not meant to represent the official position of the society.

Library of Congress Cataloging-in-Publication Data

Walsh, John J., 1913-
    Integral justice : changing people, changing structures / John J. Walsh.
        p.   cm.
    Includes bibliographical references.
    ISBN 0-88344-717-7 (pbk.)
    1. Sociology, Christian (Catholic)   2. Christianity and justice.
3. Catholic Church—Membership.   4. Church and social problems—
Catholic Church.   I. Title.
BX1753.W26   1990
261.8—dc20   90-38369
                                                              CIP

Contents

Introduction

In 1982 I wrote a short book titled *Evangelization and Justice* in which I tried to describe how people come to faith and how their faith grows—or does not grow. I noted how sad it is that many Christians in North America have little or no interest in working for justice and peace, one of the central roles of the Christian life. These "cultural Christians," good people who find religion somewhat boring, continue to go through the motions but their Christian engagement often ends with the blessing on Saturday evening or Sunday morning. If these Christians—or even a substantial number of them—became fully committed and engaged, what changes they could bring about in our world!

Justice and peace concerns have received attention from Pope John Paul II and the episcopacy throughout the world. In the encyclical *Sollicitudo Rei Socialis* Pope John Paul II made it clear that the church should be concerned with problems of justice as a part of pastoral ministry:

> The teaching and spreading of her social doctrine are part of the Church's evangelizing mission. And since it is a doctrine aimed at guiding *people's behavior*, it consequently gives rise to a "commitment to justice," according to each individual's role, vocation and circumstances (*SRS*, 41).

And in an earlier section of the encyclical, the pope made it quite clear who should be involved in this ministry:

Collaboration in the development of the whole person
and of every human being is in fact a duty of *all towards
all* . . . (*SRS*, 31).

Inspired by the leadership of the Latin American church
in the 1960s at Medellín and Puebla, justice and peace concerns have taken on a new vitality in North America. The
church even has a new vocabulary of phrases such as the
"preferential option for the poor" and "solidarity." The Bish-
ops' Conference in the United States has taken a strong position supporting justice and peace ministry in its letters on
nuclear weapons and the economy. These pastorals are no
mere collections of moral "urgings" but rather they challenge
both our military system and our economic system to do basic,
root thinking on how these systems are constructed and how
they are designed to function.

The church leadership is increasingly involved in issues
ranging from the environment to ending American interven-
tion in Central America. Activist Christians demonstrate
their feelings against the role of the United States around
the world today, calling attention to the cruel effects abroad
that often flow from our government's foreign policy or the
overseas activities of American corporations. And, yet. . . .

Why hasn't more happened? Despite a profusion of books,
resources, and study materials on justice and peace issues,
the faces in these small justice groups are the same faces.

Something is missing. Church life today calls very few to
lives of active involvement in justice and peace issues. Programs are often fragmented and results are limited. I hope
to give some guidance to pastoral ministers to take them a
step further, a step in ministry that will help them reach
"cultural Christians" and motivate them, in turn, to create
programs of justice that are integral and vital to their lives
as Christians.

Since writing my first book I have been busy lecturing,
teaching, and conducting workshops throughout the United

States and around the world on how to do evangelization in a way that will promote justice. I've concluded that we in ministry have built three-quarters of an arch, a structure that cannot stand by itself without eventually crumbling to the ground. It is similar to pushing a cart three-quarters of the way up a hill. It takes great effort just to keep the cart where it is. If we stop pushing, the cart will roll backwards. The cart will attain stability only if it gets to the crest of the hill. The arch and the cart, I feel, often symbolize our present efforts in justice ministry. Something is missing—the last quarter of the stones, or the few yards to the crest of the hill, or the spark of faith that illumines those faces in church and leads them regularly from the pews to Christian commitment and action.

In this second book I hope to give pastoral ministers a guide to help them complete the arch by increasing their understanding of the faith of Christians and by showing them some vital building "stones."

I want to thank all at Orbis Books, especially Sue Perry, for making this book possible.

CHAPTER 1

Barriers
to Integral Justice

JUSTICE MINISTRY IS a striving for the inbreaking of the Reign of God, both into our personal lives and into all the systems – political, economic, social, and religious – in which life is lived. Justice ministry seeks peace. Peace, however, is not to be equated with "quiet," which is often the goal of oppressive systems as they strive to silence the cries of the oppressed. Rather, peace is to be equated with "shalom" – life brought to its full potential under God's influence. In the words of Paul VI from *Populorum Progressio*:

> It is not just a question of eliminating hunger and reducing poverty. It is not just a question of fighting wretched conditions, though this is an urgent and necessary task. It involves building a human community where men can live truly human lives, free from discrimination on account of race, religion or nationality, free from servitude to other men or to natural forces which they cannot yet control satisfactorily. It involves building a human community . . . (47).

An integral program of justice ministry moves full circle to complete this human community of men *and women*. In this world community there are no strangers, just brothers and sisters, all of whom are meant to share in the Kingdom, the Reign of God. The Reign of God is not simply a way of speaking about the next world; instead it is the world of today as it becomes a "world completely transformed in accordance with God's plan."[1] Systemic injustice visited upon "other peo-

6

ple" different from us by life's circumstances or separated by geography tend to be beyond the scope of our psychic searchlight. Yet this is what Christ's Kingdom is all about. Truly, if we are not working for a solution, we are part of the problem.

For a number of reasons, non-integral programs often fall short of their goals. Think of last year's group of twenty devoted Christians who worked with such enthusiasm in a local food relief program. This year there will probably be only eight members, with two somewhat on the edges. A common problem in justice ministry is that we are calling on people to take a prophetic stance—a "stand"—but we are not giving them the spirituality to sustain them.

Or think of a presentation given on refugees. Twenty people showed up, two followed the discussion and seemed convinced, and ten of the twenty engaged in arguments about political issues. For most people, concerns with refugees were clearly viewed as being on the periphery of Christianity. Non-integral programs of justice ministry do not stimulate active participation by large numbers or sustain perseverance among the few who are committed. Stones are missing.

The Workers Are Few

The vast majority of people in the church are not interested in social justice. A small minority does marvelous work. Most people, however, do not see justice ministry as an integral part of what Christianity is all about. Many, in fact, are afraid of it. They don't understand it. At times, they have heard accusations against justice activity (for example, mixing religion and politics, being dupes of Communists, being unpatriotic), but they have little interest in evaluating whether these accusations are true or not. Why? Because social justice is "out there" on the periphery of Christian life. The majority of Christians feel that justice ministry is done by a small group of "radical" activists—those religious and lay people who are regularly arrested in demonstrations against nuclear weap-

ons, against the American government's support of foreign
dictatorships, or for sanctuary for refugees from these same
dictatorships. The vast majority of Christians are simply not
involved. They do not perceive that justice ministry should
play a central role in their Christian life.

Need To Understand the Hearers

The small numbers of people who work actively in justice
ministry work very hard indeed. The sowers work without
respite, and they have magnificent seed, namely, the justice
message, to sow. Many times, however, the soil does not
receive the seed. Often it doesn't seem to be a question of
good will or of the holiness of the soil. The problem seems
to lie elsewhere. For centuries it was a safe assumption that
the soil could receive the seed—and was waiting for it. That
has now become a fatal assumption. Pastoral ministers can
no longer assume that the hearer is there, waiting and listening for today's gospel message. As I will describe in Chapter
2, social ministers often assume a certain level of receptivity
on the part of listeners, a willingness to act.

Yet many "cultural Christians," Christians who are only
going through the motions, cannot hear the justice message.
They will, of course, continue to respond to the symptoms of
justice problems, such as the call to help with poverty and
homelessness. But they cannot hear the challenge to question
the systems that are the source of the problems in the first
place. Questioning the systems is psychologically threatening
because people depend on the stability of their political, economic, social, and religious systems. On the one hand, people
are quite adept at dealing with the human element. They will
tolerate a card game in which someone cheats (personal evil),
but, on the other hand, they will not play in a card game that
has unfair rules (systemic evil). People have developed a fine
nose for uncovering personal sin over the centuries, but recognizing systemic sin and admitting that one lives within an

internally flawed system is a big step to take—and a step that destroys needed security. We must remember that Christians have appropriated their faith in a certain way, at a certain level, and it is difficult to move them beyond that. Another stone is needed.

Need for a Sustaining Spirituality

A great richness of spirituality has always been attached to social justice, yet people in justice ministry, particularly if they are dealing with systemic injustice, have two great cries: "Help us, we burn out so quickly in this work. We need a spirituality that will nourish us over the long run." And they also say, "We are so enthused by the message of gospel justice, and yet most of the people to whom we speak do not hear us. Their eyes go out of focus on hearing our message. Give us a greater depth of spirituality that will touch the hearts of these good people who hear our words but not our message."

As Christians commit themselves to social ministry, it is essential that they have an ongoing deep spirituality to sustain them and to prevent the burnout that eventually hinders the progress of justice and peace programs. This spirituality must incorporate within it a pastoral strategy that enables Christians to reach not only ears but also hearts with the message of justice.

So much of the history of Christianity has been based on an interior spirituality characterized primarily by a relationship between God and an individual that leads inward toward prayer or to a contemplative lifestyle. While this spirituality may lead Christians toward holiness, it does not necessarily lead them outward. Its great richness appears to be separated by a chasm from the needs and insights of justice and peace ministry. A spirituality that supports inwardly but reaches out to others—what I call a resurrection spirituality—can introduce a new element of mysticism and new insights into the essence of ministry. Another stone for the arch.

Need for Coherence

The pre-Vatican II church had great coherence based on the theology of the Council of Trent. The beliefs and practices of Catholics around the world were uniform. They heard and repeated the same Latin liturgy and they recited a standardized catechism. Most parishes and schools were mirror images of each other. Suddenly in the mid-1960s all of this began to fall apart. As practices and beliefs changed, people no longer automatically sought Scripture, Christ, and church. It became necessary to motivate people to attend church. Great strides have since been made in motivating people, including new liturgies, new books, new prayer forms, new types of gatherings, and so forth, but coherence is often lacking. Unless there is a natural and logical connectedness and an inner accord and harmony in all aspects of Christian life, motivation alone becomes a collection of isolated urgings.

Today some in church are making a concerted effort to rediscover the 1950s and the accompanying stability of pre-Vatican II church life. Try as they might, they will never be able to turn back the clock. But they do have a point—the importance of coherence to maintain and motivate people in ministry. Social ministry must be a natural outpouring of Christian life, of prayer, of Scripture study, of worship, and of Christian community.

Need for Justice within the Church

We often see church structures that are committed to political, economic, and social justice but which, unfortunately, turn a blind eye to justice within the church. Great credibility is lost, of course, by not practicing what one preaches. Elements of patriarchy, sexism, and monopolizing of power within the church detract from an institutional voice crying for justice in other structures. But the problem goes beyond that of not always practicing what one preaches. If religious justice is not practiced, political, economic, and social justice will inevitably fail as well.

Need for Values Analysis

For centuries justice ministry has focused on curing the symptoms of problems: feeding the hungry, caring for the sick, sheltering the homeless, and so forth. Today it becomes more obvious each day that there will continue to be hungry people to be fed if the *causes* of hunger are not addressed. If Christians continue to provide shelter for the homeless, but do not ask or analyze why people are homeless, homelessness will continue.

Justice activity today must deal with the unjust systems that are the source of the symptoms of the hunger, homelessness, warfare, and environmental threats that continue to plague our world in the 1990s. In no way does this concern with unjust systems denigrate the absolute necessity to alleviate the immediate sufferings of people. But, in the long run, the symptoms will never be eliminated unless workers for peace and justice challenge the unjust aspects of these political, economic, social, and religious systems. In *Sollicitudo Rei Socialis* John Paul II calls attention to these systems by making a distinction between "sin" and the "structures of sin"; he then identifies the "structures of sin" as the "true nature of evil" (*SRS*, 37).

Christians committed to social ministry need a method to examine systems and how and why they malfunction. This type of structural analysis, which examines the flow or nonflow of power throughout some organized aspect of life, can help x-ray systems and identify and name components that operate to make them unjust. Structural analysis names those who make the decisions and those who benefit from the decisions.

A wide range of publications are available to help those

in social ministry do this type of analysis. One of the best is *Social Analysis: Linking Faith and Justice* (Holland & Henriot, Orbis, 1983). Working along with structural analysis is junctural analysis — the art of networking, which effectively links those who suffer under unjust systems with those who wish to help them.

But a stone is still missing. Before we look closely at systems, it is necessary to look at the basic values by which we live our lives. These values are embedded within all systems, whether they be economic, social, political, or religious. If the basic values are not gospel-based, the systems will not be compatible with the gospel message. An awareness of valuing within systems will provide one more tool for the pastoral minister.

The Challenge

And so we find ourselves faced with many manifestations of non-integral justice. No one is questioning the effort and sacrifice of justice ministers. But if the justice effort is applied in a fragmented way, energy is dissipated and the results, alas, are minimal.

How do we help a minority working for justice gradually become a majority? How do we help people become hearers who are ready to take the gospel message into their hearts? How do we provide social ministers with a spirituality that will sustain them? How do we provide not only motivation but coherence? How do we help a church evolve so that it is committed to religious justice as well as to political, economic, and social justice? And how does justice become not merely a double thrust of symptoms and systems, but a triple thrust of symptoms, systems, and values analysis? Our task is to change people so that they in turn can change the unjust systems in which we all live.

CHAPTER 2

Levels of Faith Appropriation

HAVE YOU WONDERED — as a pastoral minister — about the Christians who come to church, sit in the pews listening, repeat the creed and believe the "Good News," and then shake your hand at the end of the service and disappear until the following weekend? What do they do during the week? Why aren't most people involved in parish life? Why don't they feel the call to commit themselves to Christian action? Why do they walk out through the church doors and limit Christian life to an activity for Sunday mornings? And the most important question: Is there anything you can do about this?

These are good people and yet, to many of them, Christian life seems like one more business. Christians go to the garage for car repairs on Tuesday, visit Radio Shack on Thursday, the supermarket on Saturday, and then church on Sunday. They come for a service, a product, or repairs. Religion is important for these good people, yet somehow it appears like one more commodity in a commodity culture.

During the years I worked as a missioner in Japan, I carried the gospel message to people who had little or no understanding of Christianity but who were seeking something more for their lives. In a twentieth-century setting in the Far East, the dynamics of first-century, New Testament Christianity were operating once again. If Christianity responded to their needs, these seekers became followers of a new way of life. As in New Testament times they approached Christianity with a certain defensive posture lest they be "conned" or manipulated, yet they showed a willing vulnerability as they

14

listened to the longings and promptings of their hearts crying for more from life.

These converts are quite different from what I call "cultural Christians," Christians who are born into a Christian environment of family, neighborhood, and community. Converts come to faith through an internal search resulting in encounter with Christ or others. Cultural Christians come to faith through external processes within their environments.

My earlier book, *Evangelization and Justice*, analyzed cultural Christianity and described its effects on church and society. I would now like to look at the faith of these cultural Christians and then examine some deeper faith levels to help understand Christian motivation.

External Levels (Levels 1, 2, and 3)

I have outlined several levels of faith development[1] that progress from faith that is externally acquired to faith that is appropriated internally. The first level of faith is that of *vibrations* that are the deep-seated moods and attitudes about God, prayer, and church that preschoolers pick up primarily from their parents. In this process of osmosis, religious information is not nearly as important as the feelings and attitudes that are acquired. These first "vibrations" are very important because they gradually sink into the subconsciousness or unconsciousness of the person and can affect the person throughout the other levels. If, for example, the preschooler learns excessive fear—perhaps of doing wrong or of God— that attitude can manifest itself throughout life. On the other hand, deep-seated feelings and attitudes of caring may leave an individual more open to the needs of fellow humans. Most of us probably spend the rest of our lives doing remedial work on this first level.

The second level of faith development is that of *indoctrination*, which often runs from the start of formal education to the beginnings of adolescence. At this level the person is introduced to the doctrines, or better yet, the "stories" of the spiritual treasures of one's faith. "Stories" here has a broader meaning than Bible stories and basically consists of two things, the meaning of life and the way of life. The *meaning of life* for a Christian is that there is a personal God who watches over the universe. This God has taken a human face, Jesus, who is the Christ. And this Christ, although killed by the power brokers of his day, has risen from the dead and is present to us in the Scriptures and the sacraments. The *way of life* is what a Christian is challenged to do during life: the deviations from the gospel (sins) to be avoided, the aspects of the human condition to be remedied, the seeking of the fullness of life in union with Jesus and others. In sum, the *way of life* is being "members one of another." This, in turn, leads to the third level in external appropriation.

Socialization—The Christian "Parade" (Level 3)

The third level begins at adolescence and, for many people, extends right through adulthood. For centuries, the vast majority of Christians have remained at this level for the rest of their lives. They continued to grow in holiness, but it was always at this level of faith appropriation, and the holiness always had the characterics of this level. At this level, one is socialized into the faith—one is taught to do what everyone else does and to avoid what everyone else avoids. Christian life is a parade in which everyone marches in step behind a leader and which is marked first of all by uniformity.

If asked to characterize Christianity in one word without using the word "Christ," we could say "union." We seek union with Christ through love, and union with others through love, with implications naturally for individuals and society. At the third level of faith, Christian union is attained by uniformity. Indeed, one of the great tensions in the church today is whether the goals of Christianity should be attained by means of uniformity or pluriformity. Given the wide variety of cultures and circumstances in which church communities find themselves, why can there not be a wide variety of ways in which power is shared, decisions are made, theology is developed, and ministry is done?

For someone whose faith is owned or appropriated at the third level, any suggestion of pluriformity is regarded as an attack on the goal of Christianity, which is union. Although pluriformity was clearly prevalent in the New Testament churches (for example, the importance attached to circumcision or dietary laws was vastly different in the Pauline and the Palestinian churches), the marcher wants to march in the parade on a fixed route. In a desire to stay in the parade, the believer often confuses means and ends (wittingly or unwittingly), assumes the moral high ground, and attacks, often by moralizing thunderbolts, the proponent of pluriformity as a spiritual ne'er-do-well who is threatening the very goal of Christianity, namely union. The hapless person at the bottom of this moral high ground is immediately put on the defensive, judged guilty until proven innocent, and is lucky if able to emerge from this non-conversation still thought of as a loyal Christian. This is similar to saying that someone who does not support nuclear weapons does not love America.

(Many level-three persons will tolerate a fair amount of pluriformity. They may feel a certain uneasiness but they are willing to trust others who are different. A small minority, however, become "militant" threes, and are quite different from the average level-three person. The battle cry of these people is: "Not only does my faith remain at level three but your faith and every aspect of church has to go back to level three so that I feel secure." Now we smell the smoke of the inquisition.)

Uniformity is attained by following political, economic, social, or religious leaders. These attitudes of socialization apply, generally speaking, not only to religion but to all aspects of life. These leaders are followed in a non-judgmental way. People at this level of faith do not evaluate the systems (political, economic, social, or religious) in which life is lived. Understanding this characteristic is crucial to understanding why the soil cannot receive the seed—why the hearer cannot hear the message of social justice no matter how hard the messenger works.

The person at the socialization level is not naive and may realize many times that the systems in which life is lived can be exceedingly cruel. Yet, at this level, the cruelties and injustices are always ascribed to the human factor. The leaders are good people who made wrong decisions. "The president, the corporation leader, the arbiter of society, or the ecclesiastical leader is a good person but, unfortunately, he or she has signed paper A rather than paper B." The person at this parade level of faith can go even one step further. "This is not a good person who made a wrong decision but rather this is a selfish person who deliberately made a selfish decision." But what the person at the socialization level cannot do is determine that it is more than just a human factor, that the main problem comes from built-in injustices within the very machinery and the very rule book of the system itself! Systemic injustice is too threatening for the person at the third level.

Imagine playing a consciousness-raising game that goes something like this. Twenty-six players each represent a country. A, B, and C are well-to-do developed countries; D through Z are underdeveloped or developing countries. The game is played with a board somewhat like Monopoly with throwing of dice and turning over of cards. At the beginning each player has one hundred chips. Players from underdeveloped countries find their supplies of chips rapidly decreasing. But they still have faith in the game. They figure they have just been unlucky in rolling the dice or turning over cards. Even if they don't win this particular game, they are convinced they will do much better in the future. However, about three-quarters of the way through the game, it suddenly dawns upon them that the game is fixed! There is no way that players D through Z can ever win the game. Defeat is built into the very mechanics of the game. It is built into the rule book, it is built into the cards that are turned over, it is built right into the layout of the board! A, B, and C always win and D through Z always lose. (The game can be made quite insidious by insisting that players D through Z cannot play again unless they sign a document that proclaims that the game is eminently fair and is in accordance with the will of God.)

A person at the socialization or parade level of faith appropriation balks at this type of systemic evaluation. There is a psychological reluctance to step back, to view the game (or system) as a whole, and to acknowledge the systemic injustices. The Christian can have great holiness and dedication. The Christian can show great generosity in dealing with the symptoms of problems, but level-three Christians cannot hear the message of systemic justice. The "soil" cannot receive the seed.

These three levels of faith appropriation — vibrations, indoctrination, and socialization — may be called traditional or external levels. "External" does not, of course, mean shallow or without value, but rather refers to the origin of faith. Faith moves from the outside in: one is "vibed," "in-doctrinated," and "socialized." The socialized Christian's goal is to continue in the parade, not to take a different path. The level-three Christian's faith is static rather than kinetic.

Internalizing Faith

My experience has taught me that successful justice ministry is possible only when people move into an internal appropriation of faith. Their faith must begin to emanate from the inside and move outward. The faith that one has by birth, by upbringing, and by socialization must be personalized and authenticated. Just being born and raised a Christian no longer suffices. One feels impelled — both by one's own spirit and by the Holy Spirit—to take possession of one's faith in a new and deeper way. This is the level at which conversion often occurs for non-Christians, as I saw many times in Japan. At this level, if one is not a Christian, the person feels impelled to go out and become one, even if one's earlier childhood experiences, indoctrination, and socialization have been anti-Christian. At this level the Christian feels a need to account to Christ for faith, for systems of values, and for actions. Although later chapters will describe methods for pastoral ministers to help Christians move from the external parade of socialization to this deeper level of faith, it is important at this point to be aware of the differences in faith levels.

The move toward an internal appropriation of faith involves a spiritual and psychological need to go through an agonizing reappraisal. In external appropriation, one is primarily in a passive mode; in internal appropriation, the Christian switches to a more active mode of faith possession.

Support of One Model (Level 4)

The most common way in which faith is internalized is by means of small support groups in which people can enter into an *intimacy* model. As Christians move into the fourth level of faith appropriation, they experience a new closeness with Christ and often a new closeness with a small community of fellow seekers. Motivations for joining these groups vary widely, but think of these small groups within your parish: a prayer group, a study group, or a group of Christians endeavoring to delve deeper into Scripture. Often times, however, the intimacy ends at the boundaries of the small group. Although a great step has been taken forward, it is only that, *one* step. Usually such groups are open to only part of the message of social justice. Christians who are within an intimacy model will work tirelessly in a soup kitchen, for example, but will usually not question why there are so many hungry and homeless within their community. Members are capable of great sacrifice in dealing with the symptoms of injustice, but they often do not hear the message of systemic injustice.

In recent years a certain number of persons, although many fewer than those above, have begun to internalize their faith through *action* models. They hear the cries of people who have been marginated by unjust systemic violence. They understand that not only the symptoms of injustice but also the causes of these symptoms have to be addressed. As before, a great step forward has been taken, but it is only that, *one* step. If these people remain in the action model with no other support, they risk burnout. It is difficult to continue to storm the barricades of systemic injustice without the nourishment of the intimacy model where people are caring for and supporting each other. Unfortunately, many Christians remain at this level of faith, working either within a small intimate group or within one committed to action, as shown in Figure 1.

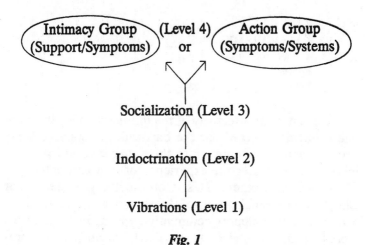

Fig. 1

Models in Creative Tension (Level 5)

It is ideal if the two groups work together, generating *creative tension* that nourishes both groups. The two groups can be compared to the two sets of muscles that form a leg or an arm. They have diametrically opposed tasks, yet they complement each other; indeed, the arm or leg could not function with only one set of muscles. If it is not practical for both groups to join together, it is imperative that each group mature by developing the opposite model and drawing on its strength as well.

It is important to understand the type of creative tension that can result from these two models, as shown in Figure 2. Creative tension does not mean a collapsing toward the middle or fence straddling; rather, creative tension is an animating and nourishing of each by the other so that the whole is greater than the sum of the parts.

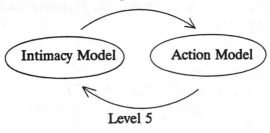

Level 5

Fig. 2

The greater the affectivity of the intimacy model, the more one is fortified to confront the barricades of systemic injustice. The more one enters into the struggle against systemic injustice, the greater the experience of love encounter with Christ and with others. This is one of the great secrets of Christianity—reaching out to others in justice action begets love within the support community, which, in turn, begets more love and action for justice. The Christian's faith appropriation has now reached that of level 5; the Christian is eager to work against both symptoms and systems and the Christian can work with perseverance, supported by faith and love through the Other and others.

Superanimation — The Goal (Level 6)

As the cycle of love spirals upward, a mystical element and a prophetic element enter in. At this level we encounter the people whom the Holy Spirit uses as magnets to draw the rest of us up through the various levels of faith appropriation. These are the ones who give us courage to climb higher and higher into the adventure and romance that Christianity can be.

These superanimated people are in touch with the heartbeat of the universe. They are change agents riding the cutting edge of the inbreaking of the Reign of God. Like Christ, they are taboo breakers, barrier breakers. Like Christ they are in trouble — from many directions. Those in power in unjust systems quickly sense that these are "dangerous" persons. Swiftly they assemble all the power at their disposal to discredit — to eliminate, if necessary — these mystic prophets. Echoes of the gospel!

A classic example in recent times is Archbishop Oscar Romero of El Salvador. Judging by external appearances, it would seem that prior to becoming archbishop, Romero was operating at a socialization or parade level of faith. No attempt is being made here to determine his personal faith or to question his holiness, yet when he became archbishop a great change took place. Viewing the abominations being visited upon the people he served, he began the journey to superanimation with all its implications of mysticism and prophetic stance. In his second pastoral letter, Romero wrote:

> If we are not faithful to this [Christian] commitment, if we do not construct a better homeland that reflects,

within our history, the final kingdom of heaven, then we
would be betraying our faith, and even betraying our
homeland. Our fidelity to Christ, the Lord of our history, will bring us the deep satisfaction of having been,
with Christ, the builders of the kingdom here in El Salvador, for the happiness of all Salvadorans.[2]

Romero's journey to bring about the Reign of God culminated with his martyrdom in the midst of the Eucharist. Once
again, echoes of the gospel.

What is fascinating about Romero is that all of this took
place in a relatively short period of time. The journey to
superanimation (level 6) for most persons is stretched out
over a much greater period of time. But Romero was in such
a pressure cooker, being assaulted by systemic power from
all sides, that his was a quick, intense journey. The descriptive
term of "superanimation" becomes flesh and blood—not only
of Romero, but of thousands upon thousands of nameless
others around the world.

Importance of Levels of Faith Appropriation

Figure 3 summarizes the progression of these levels of
faith:

↑ Superanimation (6)	
Models in Creative Tension (5)	Internal Levels
Support through Only One Model (4)	
Socialization (3)	
Indoctrination (2)	External Levels
Vibrations (1)	

Fig. 3

To ignore the levels of faith appropriation in justice ministry is tantamount to condemning oneself to an unsuccessful

justice ministry. No matter how hard the justice messenger works, no matter how compelling the justice message is, if the hearer remains at an external level of faith appropriation, much of one's efforts will be wasted. A fundamental question for ministry is how to help myself and the people I serve attain an *internal* appropriation of faith.

The level of faith appropriation is an important key to understanding motivations, actions, and commitment to justice ministry. It is not a measure of formal education, nor is it a measure of the amount of catechetical or theological information one possesses. Rather it is a measure of spiritual and psychological risk-taking. It is a measure of how much one is willing to enter into the adventure that is called Christianity. And it is a measure of courage — the courage to think new thoughts, to engage in new actions, and to pray old prayers in a new and exciting way. In writing about overcoming the "structures of sin" John Paul II noted:

> . . . one must have the courage to set out on this path, and, where some steps have been taken or a part of the journey made, the courage to go on to the end (*SRS*, 38).

As pastoral ministers, we are enablers whose task is to help people and systems reflect the Reign of God and to be step-by-step participants in the process ourselves. None of this is possible without the Holy Spirit. As we continue throughout this book to provide the stones necessary to complete the arch of integral justice, it is well to keep in mind that only the Holy Spirit can position the stones and keep them in place and only the Holy Spirit can move Christians up the scale of faith appropriation and provide them with spiritual courage. In writing to the church on evangelization, Paul VI used the following words:

> Techniques of evangelization are good, but even the most advanced ones could not replace the gentle action

of the Spirit. The most perfect preparation of the evan-
gelizer has no effect without the Holy Spirit. Without
the Holy Spirit the most convincing dialectic has no
power over the heart of man. Without the Holy Spirit
the most highly developed schemas resting on a sociological or psychological basis are quickly seen to be quite
valueless (*Evangelii Nuntiandi*, 75.3).

Ministry is a unique profession. In most other professions
it is possible to control one side of the activity. A doctor's
patient may not always listen to advice but at least the doctor
controls the medications and surgical instruments. A defense
lawyer does not control the district attorney but can instruct
a client and keep the client under control. In ministry,
however, we control neither side—neither God's grace nor
human free will is under our control. The great challenge of
our profession is to facilitate the coming together of God's
grace and human free will, to create situations whereby the
two can meet freely and deeply encounter each other. We
must not forget that justice ministry will never come alive in
actual experiences without the Holy Spirit engaging the
human spirit!

CHAPTER 3

The Christian
Discovery Process

THE PREVIOUS CHAPTERS diagnose some of the problems pastoral ministers face each day in attempting to convince Christians of the need to commit themselves to justice programs. This chapter begins a program of treatment, showing those who do ministry how to help Christians (and themselves) move from one level of faith appropriation on to another more meaningful level, a level where justice commitment naturally occurs.

As pastoral ministers we often work so hard at Christian endeavor and get so caught up in theological lists, catechetical lists, canons, organizational flow charts, and parish problems that we fail to focus on the essence of Christianity. We forget that all these lists we keep and things we do are a means to an end and not an end in themselves. We can get so caught up in the "pieces" of Christianity that we never grasp the whole. What is Christianity? Why do people turn to it? Where does faith come from? How does faith grow?

Why *do* people seek God? Thirteen years of work in Japan and thirteen other countries (six continents altogether!) has taught me that people seek God because of unfulfilled needs deep within themselves. In Japan less than 1 percent of the population is Christian. Although there are many psychological and sociological pressures against being a Christian, yet there are new Christians. In many ways, the small communities of Christians in Japan resemble New Testament Christianity in a modern setting.

Listening carefully not only to Christians but especially to non-Christians approaching Christianity can give one deep insights into the essential core of Christianity. Working in a wide variety of cultures and countries has led me to believe that I have uncovered a primal, basic Christian process that is also a core ministerial process whose steps progress in a natural order.

My intention is not to suggest that you undertake another study of your parish or school or that you hold another meeting to take stock of your resources; instead I want to introduce you to a process of *search and encounter*, a series of experiences that unfold in a specific order of development. These experiences occur as people move beyond their immediate concerns of making a living, paying bills, pursuing their careers, and raising families. Similarly, these animating experiences can give new meaning to working or to raising a family, and can form the foundation for Christian social action. What I have called the *Christian discovery process*[1] unfolds as people seek to have life "more abundantly." It is a process with its own logical order flowing from within the human heart.

The Preliminary Step

This is where we begin (or begin anew) the Christian adventure. Christian discovery is a life-long process, so we find ourselves at this stage many times in our life. It is the gateway to the primal Christian experiences.

The Primal Cry for More

All of us were created in the image and likeness of God. Even if we have food, shelter, and community, we still want and need more. We may sometimes label it "happiness" or "security" but what we want or need is often undefinable even to us. The well-known German Jesuit theologian Karl Rahner has described this missing element as an infinite longing for God and all of God's creation. We may not be able to name it or to understand it yet this infinite longing lies within each of our hearts and reflects our likeness to God. How can pastoral ministers tap this well of longing within people to lead them to an encounter with God and others? Infinities are not easy to deal with.

I'll begin with a story in the form of a dialogue.

> "I would like to be the most successful salesperson in my company."
>
> "Why? Is it the commissions?"
>
> "Well, I have no objection to money, but, to tell the truth, many more people would notice me. I'd be the center of attention."
>
> "Is that your real concern?"
>
> "Well, if many people noticed me, I'd hope that in the 'notoriety' there would also be admiration."
>
> "Right. Now once again, does it end there or is there more?"
>
> "If many people noticed me, then many would admire me and I'm really hoping that some would love me."
>
> "You want to be loved—that's what you're really seeking!"

And this is one of four needs that lie within each human heart and that help to define humankind's infinite longing for more.

The Basic Heart Wishes

The same four basic wishes of the heart unfold throughout various parts of the world.

1. We want to love.
2. We want to be loved.
3. We want to share—we want others to appreciate our experiences and emotions, and we want to enter into

the experiences and emotions of others.

4. We want to blossom—we feel that there are all kinds of potentialities within us that we would like to see come to fruition.

These basic heart wishes are not hard-and-fast, distinct categories. Each gradually blends into the next like facets on a diamond. One particular facet comes into focus and then gradually fades as the next facet appears.

These heart wishes can be expressed in an individual, personal vocabulary and also in the vocabulary of community:

Individual	*Community*
1. To love	1. To love
2. To be loved	2. To be loved
3. To share	3. To have solidarity
4. To blossom	4. To reach an ever-widening community

To love and *to be loved* is the great duplication of the love within God that lies at the core of the human heart. There is a forgetting of self and a reaching out to the other to increase the other's joy, which, in some mysterious way, increases one's own happiness. The sorrows, loneliness, wounds, and weariness of the other are to be destroyed or, at least, diminished. If nothing else can be done for the moment, one reaches out one's hands to experience a being-with and, in some way, a becoming-of the other. Ordinary life experiences become fields of opportunity. Any small concrete situation can lead to a universalizing experience and an "at-one-ness" with both others and the Other. And yet, remarkably, the others or the Other are reaching out in like manner to increase my joy, to lessen my aloneness, to enhance and give full meaning to all experiences in my life.

(It is interesting to note that people in ministry are often good at loving but poor at being loved. This seems to be an occupational hazard. We are good at giving and loving, but we are not so good at receiving or being loved. Sometimes ministry requires us to give but to receive nothing in return. Yet, in life, as a whole, this is not meant to be. To love and to be loved are reciprocal; if one breaks down, gradually the other will break down as well. If we do not have the courage to love *and* to be loved, it is easy to become a burnt-out case, loving humanity and hating humans.)

Love requires *sharing*. The word "sharing" tends to be overused today and yet its essential meaning is vital: we want others to appreciate our experiences and emotions, and we want to plunge into the experience and emotions of others. In the beginning the circle of sharing is naturally narrow: *my* family, *my* immediate community, *my* close friends, Jesus and *myself*. Sharing has to begin here but it cannot end here. Effective social and justice ministry gradually extends sharing to an ever-widening horizon. As we reach out, we seek in a special way God's *anawim*, God's nobodies, God's marginated—all those who have been pushed to the margins of the power systems (political, economic, social, or ecclesiastical). They have been pushed to the margins because of sickness, age, sex, poverty, class, culture, location, race, or lack of power. The list is endless. In a special way, we seek them out in our desire to share the experiences of God's powerless poor. And so, gradually, sharing becomes solidarity.

Loving, being loved, and sharing lead to personal growth, the *blossoming* of a person that is a lifetime project. Yet there is a paradox here, for full personal growth cannot be attained unless once again our psychic searchlight reaches out to ever-widening horizons. As we reach out to an ever-widening community that seeks to attain its full political, economic, social, and religious potential, we find the inbreaking of the Reign of God in all aspects of life. And this is the goal of Christian ministry.

Naturally, how these basic wishes of the heart are fulfilled in concrete situations will vary according to our unique personality, the circumstances of life, and the inspiration of the Holy Spirit.

Understanding the basic heart wishes is the foundation of successful justice ministry. Uncovering the God-given infinity of longing in both individual and community is the first step in uncovering the Christian discovery process. As people begin to discover their basic heart wishes (and those of an ever-widening community) and to let their religious faith unfold, *if* the logical order of the process is followed, it will evolve into a successful peace and justice ministry.

Expanding the Basic Heart Wishes

After we have identified and named these heart wishes, we need to expand them. If all we do is surface narrow heart wishes, we do more harm than we do good. Narrow heart wishes can be attained by using others—and even by using God with religious formalism. The solution is not to suppress heart wishes, but to push through to ever greater heart wishes. With expanded heart wishes, a whole new situation develops, because expanded heart wishes can only be obtained by love encounter with God and by love encounters with others.

The Primal Religious Experience

As we open our hearts, we depend on God and others to enter them. This, then, is the primal religious experience. *It is an intuitive awareness that the infinity of longing within us— as individual or community—can only be attained by loving encounters with God and with others.* Most people perceive religion as adhering to sacred customs at the institutional level. This is not to denigrate these sacred customs, but they cannot take on a vitality of their own unless they are based on this primal religious experience of the need for encounter with God and others. We keep trying to sell people on Christian practices and they haven't even bought the central idea of religion.

The Primal Cry for Help

So we attempt to have love encounters with God and others. Easier said than done. Easier written about than done! It soon dawns on us that it is not possible—by our own ability alone. And so we cry out to God for help—to love God and to love others. This primal cry for help is not to be confused with a simple intellectual assent: "Of course, I need God in all aspects of my life." No such antiseptic, academic assent will suffice. Rather, the primal cry for help is just that: a *primal* cry from one's toes, from one's whole being. Like a blind person, you can only cry out—perhaps not even in words—asking God to take your hand and lead you through. And it is a cry to God for help both in loving God and in loving others. Perched over an infinity of longing and the mystery of love encounter, nothing else will do.

The whole good news of the gospel is God's response to this primal cry for help. God's reply is an unfolding one: first, in terms of Scripture, then in terms of Christ, and then in terms of church with all its future potential.

A diagram of the Christian discovery process would look something like this:

7. Ultimate Encounter—the Fullness of the Kingdom/Reign of God

6. Encountering God and others through Eucharist

5. Encountering God and others through Church

4. Encountering God and others through Christ

3. Encountering God and others through Scripture

2. Searching (primal cry for more, primal religious experience, primal cry for help)

1. Preliminary

The Christian discovery process works like a spiral staircase, moving a person from one floor to another, steadily higher and higher. It enables people to move from one level of faith appropriation on to the next level. Level 3 "socialized" Christians can be led by pastoral ministers to examine their basic heart wishes. If they begin a search, this process may lead them into encounters with others, perhaps in intimacy or action groups. Similarly, when level 4 or 5 people (those involved with one or more models of small groups) expand their heart wishes, as did Archbishop Romero, the process of search and encounter can eventually lead them on to level 6, the stage of superanimation, the ever greater inbreaking of the Reign of God in one's life. These search and encounter experiences continue throughout the life of a Christian; they are interconnected and cumulative.

The pastoral minister's role in this constantly evolving process is to be a facilitator by recognizing the varying levels of faith appropriation and by being alert to a person's heart wishes, to those people who seem ready to search, and to those who are already searching.

Pastoral ministers do a lot of facilitating. When we observe the average parish team today, we see preoccupied people juggling fifteen ministerial plates in the air at one time. And every time they open the mail from the chancery office or attend another meeting, they do so with fear and trembling because it could mean one more item to juggle in their ministerial week. What the parish team needs is a sense of synthesis—using one process for many ministerial endeavors, one process that will assist with religious education, parish renewal, evangelization outreach, family ministry, lay leadership training, and justice and peace awareness. I feel that such a synthesis lies within the Christian discovery process of search and encounter. But the key to the process is faith—helping to understand faith and to deepen faith.

It may help to remember that Moses undoubtedly had to drag a good number of the Israelites into the desert and that some of them probably did not want to leave to search for the Promised Land. Similarly, Jesus was not born with a copy of the New Testament in his hip pocket. Jesus attained the Good News by seeking. Like each of us, Jesus had to probe, search, try things out, select, reject, try again, and keep on praying. And in so doing he gradually arrived at his message of the Kingdom. Remember also the continuing, supportive presence of the Holy Spirit, the supreme Facilitator, and pray for yourself and for those to whom you minister—that the Spirit may enter your life and theirs to help surface and expand heart wishes and to lead all persons higher and higher to the inbreaking of the Reign of God.

CHAPTER 4

Rediscovering
the Primary Role
of Scripture

SCRIPTURE CAN BE a tool of the pastoral minister as a facilitator or causer of encounter if it is read in the context of the basic heart wishes, the primal religious experience, and the seeker's primal cry for help. By using Scripture in a new way, we can reflect on the meaning of our lives and the deepest aspirations of our hearts. How do we use Scripture to cause encounters? The process is just the opposite of what we do when we use Scripture as a source of religious information and take twentieth-century people back to the first century. Now, instead, we take a first-century event and first-century people and bring them into the twentieth century. Thus the gospel story is not just about some other people long ago and far away but about me, about us, in the here and now, and about our heart wishes and how we may achieve them.

We are all familiar with the more traditional role of Scripture as a source of religious information. This is a vital role. Scripture imparts information about the God who watches over the universe, God's outreach to the Chosen People, the God who took on a human face (Jesus the Christ), and the history of the early Christians. This is a most important role of Scripture, but it is not the primary role.

In seeking to uncover the primary role of Scripture, let us focus on the gospels. What is observed here of the gospels will apply by extension to all of Scripture. Why did the formation of each gospel take anywhere from forty to sixty years from the earliest oral "Good News" beginning at Pentecost to the final written forms as we know them today? One goal, of course, was to create a body of religious information, but the final result provides us with a most spotty biography of Jesus and a history of the disciples that leave much to be desired. Clearly, this was not the primary goal. How could it take forty years to write twenty pages!

The primary goal of the gospels reflected the ministerial challenge of the early church—how to find the best way to tell the Jesus story. The story had to be told in such a way that it would bring the maximum number of people close to Christ and also bring these people close to each other through love to form a community. The primary role of the gospels then was to be an "encounter-causer," bringing about encounters of people with Jesus and with each other. Over a period of years the Good News of Jesus was worked and re-worked in oral and written forms until the best ministerial tool resulted. The final forms, as we know them today, were the best pastoral tools produced by the early church com-munities.

As pastoral ministers, how can we use the Scriptures in this way as "encounter causers"? My best efforts have involved a two-fold process:

1. Surfacing "corresponding experiences,"
2. Allowing for a time delay.

Surfacing "Corresponding Experiences"

"Corresponding experiences" is put in quotation marks because it has a special meaning. It does not mean "identical" or even necessarily "similar" (in the sense that if I am sick, I look up passages about people being ill). Rather, it has a deeper meaning. It is not the surface story or the concrete details that are important. We must go deeper than that and uncover the corresponding *dynamic*. For instance, I am as close to despair as were some gospel characters. I experi-ence great anger—as did Christ. Hope, joy, infinite longing, searching, the desire to love, to be loved, to share, to have

solidarity, to grow as individual and community, to reach out
to others, to experience the inbreaking of the Reign of God —
the list is endless.

Consider the situation of the early New Testament communities. They were small, only a tiny minority of the population. Great sociological and psychological pressures — not
to mention outright force — were brought to bear on them.
Yet in a way their very smallness was their strength because
it allowed for a great deal of interaction. Gathered among
themselves, not as ghetto but as leaven, they constantly
sought to influence, enable, and empower each other, new
followers who were constantly entering the community, and,
in some small way, the population at large.

They acted as leaven through the Jesus story. But no mere
telling of the biography of Jesus would suffice. Somehow the
past had to be made present. No mere drawing of "lessons"
from good stories would suffice. The Good News becomes
"Good News" only when it brings forth not only goodness
but newness. How then to make the past present? How to
draw a newness from old stories?

At an intuitive level, under the guidance of the Spirit of
Christ, the early Christians realized that the Jesus story *had*
the power to bring about new encounters of love in their lives.
The Jesus of the past could act in the present. The gospel
stories were empowered by a Risen Christ who was not limited by time or by geography. Gradually the Christians came
to understand the power of the gospel as encounter causer.
It could bring about new encounters of love with Jesus and
with others. In striving to unleash this power, the early Christians came to realize that the biographical details were of
little importance and, in fact, at times could be a hindrance.
Rather, what was important was to enter into the depths of
the historical account and to draw from it a primal action or
attitude that was also taking place in their lives as individuals
or as a community. In short, they learned to surface "corresponding experiences." And so they worked and re-worked

the gospel stories with this in mind. They also came to understand that this same surfacing of corresponding dynamics was possible with both the Hebrew Scriptures and the other writings of what would be known as the New Testament.

We can find, for example, a "corresponding experience" in the story of Pontius Pilate from the Gospel of John (18:33-19:16). Pontius Pilate did not really want to execute anybody. He just wanted everyone to give in a little, to be reasonable, so he could work out a settlement where there would be something for everybody. The way he saw it, he basically was faced with a failure to communicate. He wanted to be fair, but not *too* fair; he had to be cautious because too much "fairness" could damage his career. The Jews were so stubborn, and this Jesus wasn't giving him any help. What did Jesus expect—one hundred percent justice? Didn't Jesus realize that governors have to keep a lot of people happy?

Today, anyone who cannot identify with Pilate is probably very short on self-knowledge. We are all born compromisers, and we have all become experts in rationalization and self-deception. We all know that temptation to wash our hands of an issue when we should take a stand.

Or examine the story of Jesus telling his closest followers that he must go to Jerusalem to suffer at the hands of his enemies (Matt. 16:21-28). Peter tried to talk Jesus out of it. Jesus lashed out at him, calling him a devil, and told him to get out of his way. Then Jesus described the cost of discipleship as nothing less than carrying a cross. We are told that the disciples "understood none of these things; this saying was hid from them, and they did not grasp what was said." Of course, *we* understand. Or do we? Do we really accept Jesus' terms, or do we hope to work out some kind of deal? Maybe a smaller cross, or a more comfortable one? The words of Jesus, when we really listen to them, are just as blunt and uncompromising, and just as hard to accept as the first time he said them at Caesarea Philippi. And if we are as dense as the disciples, it is probably for the same reason:

they did not want to listen to talk of suffering and death. But when they stopped listening to what was painful to them, they also failed to hear what Jesus said about resurrection.

Almost every story in the gospels deals with some dynamic at play within us today—we make poor judgments, we yield to temptation, we take pride in self—the list is endless. But by reading Scripture in this manner, we can experience what seems to have happened to so many people who came in contact with Jesus of Nazareth. In his presence they were invited to see themselves as they really were, and to get a glimpse of what they could be. Are we so different today? If we look to Scripture for encounter with God, we *will* find God there.

The Time Delay

Once the "corresponding experience" is surfaced, do not expect immediate results. Although the effects of reading or hearing the gospel or Scripture might be immediate, they will more likely come after some delay—an hour, a day, a week, or a month. We cannot program the Holy Spirit or the human spirit.

In the early church it was necessary to personalize and authenticate one's faith in order to enter the Christian community. Membership was by adult conversion at an internal level of faith appropriation. In order to facilitate conversion, Scripture was used primarily as an encounter causer and secondarily as a source of religious information. Over the centuries, especially after Christianity became well established, Scripture became used primarily as a source of religious information for its indoctrinating and socializing effects. Scripture as encounter causer retreated into the background.

We are so accustomed to using Scripture as a source of religious information (usually with immediate results) that we are programmed to expect instant results. Without realizing it we have boxed in the power of Scripture to fifteen- or twenty-minute periods. Once the time-delay effect of Scriptures is recognized, the power of Scripture is extended. When the Holy Spirit and the human spirit finally come together, the result can be spectacular—a new and deeper encounter of love with Christ, and a new and deeper encounter of love with others. Immediate results are gratifying to those in ministry because we quickly see the results of our efforts. It is good to keep in mind, however, that immediate results are generally short-lived while time-delayed results can be life-changing.

If the final ministerial goal is to help people attain the socialization or parade level of faith appropriation, using Scripture for the most part as a source of religious information may well suffice. However, at this level people do not evaluate the structures in which life is lived. Successful justice ministry requires helping people move on to the internal levels of faith appropriation. This use of Scripture as encounter causer now becomes imperative.

There might be a lurking suspicion that all of this smacks of an anti-intellectual approach to Scripture. But it goes without saying that the more one knows of "source criticism" (life setting of Jesus), "form criticism" (life setting of the early Christians), "redaction criticism" (life setting of the evangelist's community), and contemporary literary forms, the better one will be able to facilitate the surfacing of these "corresponding experiences."

For Scripture to work well as encounter causer it can no longer be treated in isolation, which happens many times when Scripture is used as a source of religious information. For Scripture to come alive as encounter causer, it must enter into the first stages of the Christian discovery process—the primal cry for more, the primal religious experience, and the primal cry for help. And Scripture must flow on to the later stages of the Christian discovery process that will be described in the following chapters.

Scripture as Encounter-Causer—Other Techniques

Uncovering the Silence in Scripture

Scripture contains not only a divine element but also a human element. It is the word of God but, even so, conditioned by historical circumstances, it is couched in the words of men (exclusive language deliberately used). As a whole, the books of the Bible were written by men for men in a world controlled by men. There is an underside to all of this that has to be uncovered—the silence and silencing of women. Both in the composition of Scripture and in the interpretation of biblical events within Scripture, women have been suppressed or, if not suppressed, highly marginalized. For the Scriptures to truly work as an encounter causer—or as a source of religious information, for that matter—we have to fill in the silence. We must re-explore our Christian roots and uncover our hidden history. There is a great paradox here. Listening closely to Scripture will, of course, help us to better understand the marginated of the world. But the marginated of the world will, in turn, help us to better understand Scripture—Scripture spoken and Scripture silent.

The work of uncovering the silence will be endless. One small suggestion might be worth considering. Reflect on the following passages from the Wisdom literature:

Proverbs 3:13-18, 4:5-13, 8:1-9:6
Baruch 3:15-4:4
Sirach 1:1-18, 4:11-18, 14:20-15:10, 24:1-31
Wisdom 6:12-21, 7:7-8:21, 9:9-18
Song of Songs: person seeking and person being sought.

With the exception of the *Song of Songs*, these are beautiful lyric passages in praise of wisdom. What were the authors trying to do? There is a real possibility that they were trying to bring out the feminine aspects of God. By this, I do not mean feminine and masculine stereotypes. "Feminine aspects" is used here in the sense that God is an infinite phenomenon and all descriptions, modifiers, and analogies are going to tell us a little more about who God is. Through the centuries, the God that had been unfolding had been a rather one-sided God; these passages were an attempt to rectify the balance and uncover more of the fullness of God.

As you read these passages, every time you see "wisdom," "she," or "her," insert in mental parentheses the word, "God." See if you do not get a greater insight into who God is. Much more important, see if you do not experience Scriptures as an encounter causer with new and deeper experiences of God. For example:

Blessed are those who have discovered wisdom [God],
 those who have acquired understanding!
Gaining her [God] is more rewarding than silver,
 her [God's] yield is more valuable than gold.
She [God] is beyond the price of pearls,
 nothing you could covet is her [God's] equal.
Prov. 3:13-15

Or,

Wisdom [God] brings up her [God's] children
 and cares for those who seek her [God].
Whoever loves her [God] loves life,
 those who seek her [God] early will be filled with joy.
Whoever possesses her [God] will inherit honor,
 and wherever he walks, the Lord will bless him.
Sir. 4:11-13

In the *Song of Songs* there are two basic roles: the person seeking, and the person being sought. Sometimes the seeker is male and the sought-after is female. At other times, the seeker is female and the sought-after is male. Assign all the seeker roles to God and all the sought-after roles to yourself and let the gender fall where it may.

Then reverse the roles. Assign all the seeker roles to yourself and all the sought-after roles to God. Nineteen out of twenty verses will probably not mean much at all, but the twentieth verse may illuminate a new aspect of God or God's relationship to you. See if you do not get a deeper insight into who God is. Again, and much more important, see if it does not result in new and deeper experiences of God.

The Gospels: Reflection on a Ministry Cut Short

People sometimes claim that on examining the gospels they find many more passages relating to personal holiness than to systemic holiness. It all sounds a little mechanical but let's take the argument at face value. All the systems of Jesus' day were to a greater or lesser extent part of the Roman Empire web and Rome was dedicated to the status quo. Jesus began his ministry in Galilee with individuals, speaking to them about the implications of the Reign of God in their personal lives. The Roman web was shaken, if ever so slightly at first. "This fellow bears watching!" To use anachronistic terms, a dossier was initiated, reports were entered into the computer, agents (overt and covert) were sent out to observe and at times harass. It all sounds so familiar!

Still young in his ministry, Jesus moved to Jerusalem, the center of Roman occupation where the various threads of power came together. How often we read the gospels and forget that they took place in *occupied* territory. How often we read the gospels and forget that their final form took place in communities hoping to be accepted—or at least tolerated—by Rome; hence, they played down the vital role of Roman power. Would that a clearer record of the earlier gospel forms were available. One suspects they would have been much blunter regarding Roman power. Jesus moved to the center of power to concentrate more on the implications of the Reign of God regarding systemic power. The operative word here is "began," for suddenly he was killed. Jesus only got from A to E in his ministry. If he had been allowed to get to X, Y, and Z, it is likely that the Roman web would never have been the same. The gospels then are a reflection on a ministry cut short—very short.

Perhaps the greatest trial for Jesus' disciples was not that he was killed but that he was killed so early. The disciples had to identify the trajectory initiated by Jesus and extend it. The same challenge faces us today. If we neglect Jesus' call to Kingdom and turn a blind eye to systemic injustice, the coming of God's Reign is postponed. Action groups focusing on systemic sin and injustice can gain strength and support for their work through reflection on this aspect of Jesus' ministry, and how they in turn are called to follow in his path to extend his ministry.

The Koan *Effect of Scripture*

Another technique we can use to open up Scripture is the *koan*, a Buddhist term for an unusual and mysterious riddle, but a riddle that has no answer on the usual rational, logical level. For example, "What is the sound of one hand clapping?" This leads to great anxiety for a time—until one allows oneself to be jolted from the usual rational level into an intuitive level. Often intuition is not well understood in the Western world. It is regarded as a glorified emotion—floating, fragmentary, and fragile—if not downright "spacey." In any case, intuition is definitely second-rate to reason and logic.

In the Orient, however, (and, by the way, Christianity's roots *are* oriental) and in many of the so-called primitive cultures of the world, intuition is regarded differently. Intuition, which is seen as reason and logic operating at a higher level, is a key to knowledge. To couch it in Western terms: intuition is the intellect aided by the will and the emotions leaping to the final conclusion (of insight and commitment) *without explicitly* going through the intermediate stages of rational development. The operative words above are "with-

out explicitly," for intuition does touch these rational intermediate steps in an implicit way. The role of traditional
reason, then, is to explicate the intermediate stages and verify
the final conclusion of insight and commitment already
arrived at by intuition. This, in turn, sets the stage for the
next intuitive leap. Figure 4 shows a diagram of this process.

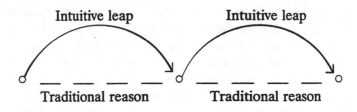

Fig. 4

Intuition and traditional reason do not work at cross pur-
poses. Rather, they work in dialectical harmony, each furthering the other. But it is intuition that begins the grand
adventure.

But what are the ministerial implications of all this? In the
past, when the ministerial goal was the socialization or parade
level of faith appropriation, a primarily traditional rational
way of doing ministry sufficed. But if people are to move on
to an internal level of faith appropriation — a prerequisite for
successful justice ministry — then ministry at the intuitive level
must be an integral part of one's endeavors. It is at this intuitive level that the Holy Spirit and the human spirit come
together. It is at this intuitive level that God's grace and
human free will come together. It is at this intuitive level that
the commitment to encounter Christ and to encounter others
is made. And yes, it is at this intuitive level that people fall
in love!

And so we come to the *koan* effect of Scripture. Practically
all of Scripture is open to the *koan* effect. Some passages,
such as the Sermon on the Mount or the parables, are more

pregnant with possibility than others. Consider, for example, some passages from the Sermon on the Mount.

> "You have heard how it was said, *eye for eye and tooth for tooth*. But I say this to you: offer no resistance to the wicked. On the contrary, if anyone hits you on the right cheek, offer him the other as well; if someone wishes to go to law with you to get your tunic, let him have your cloak as well. And if anyone requires you to go one mile, go two miles with him. Give to anyone who asks you, and if anyone wants to borrow, do not turn away" (Matt. 5:38-42).

These instructions of Jesus can place the reader squarely on the horns of a dilemma. If the instructions are followed *literally*, Christians could become the "patsies" for all sorts of devious con artists. Similarly, systematic exegesis can turn these instructions into pious nothings. But consider the *koan* technique, which presents another approach, recognizing that all issues cannot be solved on the level of exegesis and that insight can take place as well at the intuitive level. Applying the *koan* technique of intuition to the Sermon on the Mount might take the following direction:

> There are so many homeless people. I'm not really solving the problem by giving this homeless man my shirt. I'm not doing enough. This is going to require some commitment from me and some life change on my part. This is a challenge of the Spirit and shows the Spirit's capacity to call people — and me.

Throughout much of the history of Christianity the great *koan* has been the cross. Coming face to face with actual suffering and sin — with the presence of evil in the world — often undermines our theoretical understanding that God draws good from evil. In real situations of life and death, the mind and heart freeze. God's ability to create good from evil and to bring salvation through the cross cannot be approached at just the rational level. Understanding and absorbing such a mystery requires an intuitive leap from the believer. The resurrection is an even greater *koan*, and a *koan* that Christianity must tap to understand the infinite treasure that lies hidden there. We shall begin to explore this *koan* in Chapter 6.

Sharing Our Reflections on Scripture

More and more today, personal testimony is becoming an integral part of ministry. "Don't tell me what Jesus is going to do for me. Tell me what Jesus *has done* for you," is the challenge often heard by those in ministry. Personal testimony, however, is a two-edged sword. At times, it is necessary to speak in the first person ("I," "me," "my"), but if you do it continually you run the risk of becoming boring—or self-centered. How can we give personal testimony without continually slipping into the first person?

Look through the passages on which you are going to give your reflection (for example, homily, catechetical reflection, religion class). See if some verse or verses don't leap out at you. Why? Because they have already acted as encounter causers in your life. Even if these verses have not yet led to actual encounter experiences, there is an intuitive feeling about certain verses. You sense that they are going to lead to encounter experiences in your future. Like miniature time bombs, you can hear them ticking! Concentrate your reflection on these verses. You may well stay in the third person ("he," "she," "they," "them"), but even so people will sense the personal element of how Scripture has been experienced as an encounter causer in your own life.

The Fullness of the Good News in Scripture: God among Us as Christ

Why did God come among us? The traditional answer is that Jesus came to save us, to redeem us, to liberate us from the sins we have personally committed as individuals. This is spectacular news indeed, but the Good News is even "gooder" than we think it is. Scripture as encounter causer can lead us to meet and experience a Christ who has come to save us not only from personal sin but also from the systemic sin incorporated in our political, economic, social, and religious systems.

So why did God come among us? God, through Jesus, came to encounter each of us personally through love, and to enable each of us to encounter others through love. God took on the full meaning of human existence through Jesus who loved all persons and who shared their hunger, sickness, and pain. Jesus became human and thereby dignified all human existence. But as God became human in Jesus, God also entered into our human society with all of its unjust systems. Jesus' encounters with others show clearly that God is also loved and worshiped through doing justice, showing mercy, breaking bread with others, and restoring broken relationships. Encounters with the "least" of God's people are encounters with God.

In this way Christ becomes *the* Encounter Causer and we begin to experience a Christ who liberates us from personal *and* systemic sin and who leads us to love others. Christ does not just liberate us *from* something; Christ also liberates us *for* something. And so the fullness of the Good News of God among us is a Christ who comes to:

save
redeem
liberate us

from: personal sin   *for*: love encounter
systemic sin

In this extended Good News of incarnation lies the foundation for a modern spirituality of ministry and mission. Jesus comes to us in love as one of us; as we respond to Jesus in love, we also reach out in love to others, choosing to share their lives.

As people move from an external to an internal appropriation of faith, they need new guidelines for their spiritual life. Let us recall the various levels of faith appropriation:

- Superanimation (6)   Internal
- Models in Creative Tension (5)
- Support of Intimacy or Action Model (4)
- Socialization (3)   External
- Indoctrination (2)
- Vibrations (1)

Action of Jesus in the Intimacy Model

As people move from external to internal appropriation of faith, they generally choose one of two ways or models for internalizing their faith: the *intimacy* model or the *action* model. As seen in Chapter 2, the intimacy model stresses an at-one-ness with Christ and a small group of fellow seekers. The action model stresses service to those marginated by unjust systems and a critique of those systems themselves. It seems that many more opt for an intimacy type of model than those who opt for some type of action model.

Those who opt for an intimacy model hear this part of the expanded Good News of God among us:

Jesus came to: save
redeem
liberate us

from: personal sin   *for:* love encounters

The Good News of this intimacy model is that people experience Christ as *the* Encounter Causer in their lives. Christ comes alive in their lives. There is a great mutual openness and caring within the small group. The bad news is that all of this is usually limited to the confines of the small group.

Action of Jesus in the Action Model

Those who enter into the action model hear this part of the expanded Good News of God among us:

> Jesus came to: save
> redeem
> liberate us
>
> —not only *from* personal sin
> —but also *from* systemic sin

The Good News of the action model is that people experience a great at-one-ness with God's *anawim*. These people, "the least," are no longer just a sad story in the daily news but truly become one's sisters and brothers. Gradually there dawns an awareness that not only the symptoms of these persons' plight must be addressed, but also the systems that are the sources of their marginalization. The world and, surprisingly, the very systems themselves praise those who deal with the symptoms of these problems. To critique the systems, however, is to expose oneself to suspicion from the world at large and to vicious retribution from the systems themselves. Because of this, the bad news is that the action model cannot long endure of itself and will burn out quickly without an intimate support group.

Jesus in the Intimacy-Action Spiral

It is obvious then that both the intimacy model and the action model need each other for fulfillment. A person must pass from a transitional level of internal faith appropriation to an integrated level of internal faith appropriation. The foundation for a modern spirituality of ministry and mission is to be found at this level of faith appropriation. Here the intimacy model and the action model are in creative tension with each other. Here the fullness of the Good News of God among us becomes operative:

> Jesus came to: save
> redeem
> liberate us

> — not only *from* personal sin
> — but also *from* systemic sin   — *for:* love encounters

It is important to remember that at the integrated level of internal faith appropriation there is no mere mixing of the intimacy and the action models, nor a mere collecting of the "parts" of the fullness of the Good News of God among us. Rather all of these are in creative tension with each other. Love encounter begets liberating activity against systemic (and personal) sin. Liberating activity begets love encounter. Intimacy begets action. Action begets intimacy.

With Christ, God among us, as impetus, the intimacy-action spiral has infinite possibilities. Christ, the Encounter Causer, becomes the cornerstone of all community, including friendship, family, parish, religious groups, and justice endeavor. The superanimation level of faith appropriation opens up, with its mystical potential and its prophetic stance. Each of these, in turn, are in creative tension and beget one another. With Christ as the foundation, a new world of spirituality opens.

CHAPTER 5

The New Spirituality

THE CHRISTIAN DISCOVERY process continues to unfold as we experience Scripture as encounter causer, and Scripture, in turn, helps us to experience Christ as liberator and *the* Encounter Causer. This process facilitates growth in faith appropriation and permits a new spirituality that values and affirms our humanity and that opens us up to life rather than shutting us off from it. More often than not, the older spirituality was directed toward achieving personal holiness and led its advocates away from society. This new spirituality—what I call a resurrection spirituality—should strengthen people inwardly but lead them outward. If we want to create effective programs of social ministry, we ourselves must attempt this new spirituality along with the people we serve.

Donal Dorr has described spirituality as the place in which God speaks to us. Dorr adds that our spirituality lies in the way we think and act, and in what shapes and moves us. This spirituality does indeed lead us outward:

> I see the hand of God not merely in my own life but also in the lives of my friends. I can be led on to believe that God's plan of salvation is all-embracing—it touches the lives of nations as well as individuals. My trials, my rescue, my being led into a more authentic pattern of living, my whole destiny—all these are fitted by God into the destiny of my people and of all peoples).[1]

Spirituality deepens or is strengthened through the work of the Spirit in much the same way as faith. As pastoral ministers we can also be facilitators of spirituality by understanding the role played by others, the nature of prayer, and the continuing challenge this new spirituality offers.

Spirituality through Intimacy

Spirituality grows through our encounter with Jesus as we experience Christ as the ultimate personality—one fully alive, in touch with God and all of God's creation. Our destiny then is to imitate Christ as we strive for ultimate personal growth, encounter, and solidarity with others.

Our own endeavors alone are insufficient, but in a Christ-filled universe all is attainable. True personal growth, however, presents a paradox. If we fill up with only *personal* growth there is the incipient danger of becoming merely "full of ourselves." The challenge is to fill up *and* to empty out at the same time. For into this vacuum comes a Christ who empowers us to love others. This empowerment, in turn, leads us to experience Christ in others, a Christ who empowers them to love us. Gradually we begin to experience ourselves in others and others in us—all loving Christ. We no longer end with our skin. Imperceptibly the entire envelope of the whole universe begins to become our new skin. The wonder of this empowerment is that in no way does it diminish our individuality, our uniqueness, or our personhood. On the contrary, intimacy begets personal growth and personal growth begets intimacy. We are moving toward our destiny: the ultimate "you" or "me" experiencing ultimate intimacy with Christ and with others.

The Role of Prayer

Prayer then becomes an experience of intimacy-presence. For as long as we can remember, we have been challenged to "pray always," but somehow it never seems to work. How can we go through the thousand and one activities of daily life and continually think of God?

At times there is need for "busy" prayer filled with words and at other times there is need for "busy" prayer filled with ideas. But there is also a great need for "open" prayer when we attempt to open up—to create a vacuum—so that Christ can come in. In peak moments of prayer we experience ourselves filled with Christ and all is well. However, "nature abhors a vacuum" and as soon as we cease feeling filled with Christ, we get anxious. We feel the need to fill the vacuum with many words and pious ideas. If we don't do this, distractions enter our prayer accompanied by psychic alarm bells warning us that our spiritual life is going amiss. Tension sets in and we set out to work, to play, to do anything rather than stay involved in tension-filled open prayer.

Once again, what to do? One approach is to turn the problem on its head and let the so-called "distractions" enter into our open prayer. As people and events and all the clutter of daily life come tumbling in, let us realize that they are entering into a situation saturated with Christ. Whether we *feel* Christ's presence at the moment or not, Christ is present and the situation is Christ-filled. This prayer may be messy but nobody ever said we had to get an "A" for neatness in prayer. Surprisingly, this experience, disjointed though it may be at first, can gradually lead to a calmness, a peace, a fullness that is thoroughly unexpected. The expected dichotomy between "exterior" and "interior" in the spiritual life gradually gives way to a more holistic experience. Past, present, and future are more closely intertwined under Christ, and under Christ distant events and distant people come closer together.

And so we live life and encounter the people, the events, and all the clutter of daily existence, but the Christ-filled experience of prayer has transformed them into old friends. Prayer and activity complement each other and gradually become one. Perhaps the injunction to "pray always" is not so impossible after all. We begin to experience an at-oneness with Christ, other people, and all of creation. In this at-one-ness lie the seeds of the inbreaking of the Reign of God.

Spirituality through Action

The at-one-ness with Christ and all of creation lead us naturally into action, but action in a new way. Like Christ's life, action now no longer takes place in *chronos* but in *kairos*. *Chronos* is life taking place in the ordinary flow of time. *Kairos*, on the other hand, is time viewed as a series of Spirit-filled opportunities.

Chronos is the time of habit. That's good news and bad news. Some habits liberate; we can tie our shoelaces, use a knife and fork, do a thousand and one things almost effortlessly, thanks to habit. But habit can also enslave. Consider the banality of evil—especially systemic injustice. We get so used to seeing it that we *no longer see it*. The great strength of the status quo is that it *is*. If it *is*, if it exists, then it must be. It becomes a part of the fabric of daily living and systemic violence goes unchallenged. Habit is so powerful that, at times, even the enchained will seek to enchain others. They will bypass the primal question, "What is the real issue here?" (systemic injustice) and quibble over a point of procedure within the system. They will do anything but question the system itself.

And so *kairos*, the time of Spirit-filled opportunities, must come into play. If ever there was a time for a *kairos* view of time, it is now. For we are an "exodus generation," a people living in a time of massive change required by the confluence of a series of events. The people of our generation are called to make a quantum leap in response to these events.

To date, in our religious tradition, there have been only five exodus generations:

1. the original exodus people,
2. the generation that threw in its lot with an itinerant missioner called Jesus of Nazareth,
3. the extended generation that joined an under-

ground, outlawed catacomb-church gathered around
the memory of a Jesus who was condemned as a proto-
revolutionary and blasphemous heretic, yet a Risen
Christ,

4. the extended generations of the sixteenth and sev-
enteenth centuries who were called to face a world of
discovery (geographical, scientific, philosophical, and
theological),

5. the present generation who for the first time in
almost 1,700 years of Christianity is being called to live
at the same level of faith appropriation as the New Testament generations.

The world we live in and the world our faith must confront
is a world of global change: changes in Eastern Europe, in
South Africa, in Central and Latin America, in the North-
South conflict, in the world economy, in the destruction of
our global environment, and in our churches. Instant communications allow us to see challenges to sexism, classism,
and racism from every corner of the world. *Kairos*, the time
of Spirit-filled opportunities, requires that all the systems by
which we organize life be subjected to the scrutiny of the
gospel. As we prepare for the year 2,000 and beyond, Christ
challenges our generation to achieve a level of faith that
demands not only personal holiness but also systemic holiness. In the words of Donal Dorr,

> We need to envisage an alternative world, one where
> Kingdom values are embodied not only in the political
> and economic structures of society but also in the whole
> tradition and way of life.[2]

Living a *kairos* life is not always easy. The virtues of living
in a framework of *chronos* in Egypt with an externally
acquired faith can well become vices during an exodus into
a desert, and what were considered vices in Egypt can be the

virtues of desert life. Although unquestioning loyalty, complete docility, and total acquiescence to the many systems of life may work well in a non-exodus time, an exodus generation cannot afford their luxury. As with the original exodus people, our exodus generation is challenged to evaluate all the systems (political, economic, social, religious) in which life is lived. Legal may not always coincide with moral. Power may not always coincide with authority. The core value of the myth may not always coincide with the myth's popular or even twisted interpretation. The "sayings" (orthodoxy) may not always coincide with the "doings" (orthopraxis). All systems have to be evaluated in each of these categories.

An exodus endeavor of evaluating these systems implies certain occupational hazards. Led by the Spirit, Jesus initiated such an endeavor and was quickly condemned as a danger to political, economic, social, and religious stability. And so he died as a villain *outside* the walls. Once a person takes a prophetic stance against unjust structures, the systems are quick to employ Orwellian tactics against that person. Solution becomes problem and problem becomes solution. Although it is often the unjust systems themselves that are the real problem, the prophet who comes bearing a solution may quickly be labeled the "problem." The "solution" of the systems is to denigrate or, if need be, to eliminate the "problem," in this case, the prophet. And, sadly, this action is usually taken on behalf of the members, who are often also the victims, of the unjust systems.

As each Good Friday comes around, many of us Christians pull together the courage to tell Jesus that we are willing to die with him. But we often neglect the more important issue: Are we open to the possibility of dying with a Jesus who is a political, economic, social, or religious villain?

The Search for "Certainty" or the Search for the Whole Truth?

Jesus initiates the inbreaking of the Reign of God and with it comes the mandate to search for the whole truth until the fullness of time. Such a mandate calls for endless struggle. People and systems are often tempted to settle for much less. This is the lure of "certainty," which has a special meaning in this context. It is the taking of a partial truth and proclaiming it as the whole truth. Recall the old story of the elephant and the three blind men. One puts his hands on the elephant's trunk and proclaims the elephant is like a snake. Another put his hands on the elephant's side and proclaims the elephant to be like a wall. The third puts his hands on one of the elephant's legs and affirms the elephant is like a tree. Each has attained a partial truth but none attained the fullness of reality, the whole truth. Which of the three discoveries will the blind men agree on? They have two options:

1. Proclaim the discoveries already made and continue the search, or

2. Suppress the creative tension created by three discoveries, proclaim one of the partial truths as "official" (e.g., the elephant is like a tree), and view with suspicion, if not outright hostility, the other discoveries.

Notice that the second option does not proclaim a falsehood; rather a partial truth is proclaimed to be the whole truth and thus a degree of "certainty" is attained.

Throughout much of history people have selected the second option. Why? Because "certainty" offers security to both individual and system. As long as one's spiritual life rests on a traditional (or external) level of faith appropriation this "certainty" has a special allure. Often without realizing it, people judge the success of their spirituality (their attempt at holiness) by the criterion of "certainty." Systems uphold "certainty" because "certainty," in turn, upholds the status quo of the systems. In the security of a closed and "certain" system — in which "there is a place for everything and everything has its place" — a great deal of reality is bypassed.

This form of "certainty," however, will not suffice in an exodus time such as ours when millions of believers are moving on to an internal appropriation of faith. Today the new criterion for judging spiritual progress (holiness) must be the presence of ambiguity—the ambiguity of struggle and search and the ambiguity of unanswered questions. People and systems are now faced with a continual challenge: to settle for a partial truth or to continue to search for the whole truth.

Do they settle for:	or Do they search by means of:
—the easily measured	—the nuanced
—the all powerful leader	—consensus representatives
—endless rules	—guiding principles

Living with ambiguity, especially in terms of spirituality, is like walking on a razor's edge. It is an uncomfortable challenge. We have a tendency to jump off quickly to one side or the other. Yet a sustaining and stimulating spirituality requires an effort from us to walk that thin line and to live in creative tension with what is on both sides of the razor's edge:

—striving for ultimate personal growth	—striving for ultimate encounter
—ongoing intimacy	—ongoing action
—prayer as encounter with God	—prayer as encounter with others
—maintaining the habits that liberate	—freeing ourselves from the habits that enslave
—affirming where legal and moral coincide	—challenging where legal is not moral; affirming when moral is not legal
—affirming where power and authority coincide	—challenging where power lacks authority; affirming where true authority lacks power

| —affirming when "say-
ings" and "doings"
coincide | —challenging when
"doings" do not
match "sayings" |

As we look at the choices above, our task appears decep-
tively easy. "Yes, yes. I'm for all of those things—on both
sides. It's just a question of balancing out a certain amount
from each side." But no, that is not what should be done.
That is simple fence-straddling, not walking or running along
the razor's edge. The two sides should not collapse toward
the middle; rather they should feed each other. Each empowers and animates the other so that there is an ever-increasing
intensity and commitment on both sides culminating in the
mystical and the prophetic.

A spiritual life as a walking or running along the razor's
edge is impossible even for a moment by one's own effort
alone. Many Christians find the razor's edge too frightening
and look for methods to practice spirituality off the razor's
edge. The methods are numerous, but to name but a few:

- —blind allegiance to an individual leader
- —blind allegiance to a set of rules
- —blind allegiance to a set of *chronos* habits,
- —blind and literal allegiance to a twisted interpretation
  of life-giving myth

It is important to note that each of these methods may
well entail great sacrifice, and many people will resort to them
because they expect sacrifice in the spiritual life. For them,
sacrifice is often preferable, and more comfortable than
ambiguity. So it is with fear and trepidation that we climb
once more onto the razor's edge. We must remember that
Jesus the Christ did not die, rise, and go away. The Risen
Christ is present for us now, to be with us and to support us.
As the Risen Christ supports us on the razor's edge of search
and ambiguity, we encounter another paradox of faith. In the

ambiguity of the challenge to work for the inbreaking of the Reign of God, we may discover a different form of "certainty"—the certainty of faith, love, and hope in the Risen Christ. The church, the body of Christ, can provide help.

CHAPTER 6

Church as Easter-Pentecost Process

AS SPIRITUALITY helps Christians spiral upwards in faith, the adventure of Christian discovery continues. We belong to a church and we seek a Christ who is in the church. This brings us face to face with a very elemental question: What is church? Christ's life on earth culminated in two cosmic events: Easter and then Pentecost. If we can penetrate more deeply into the fullness of the good news of Easter and the fullness of the good news of Pentecost, we should then be able to arrive at the core of the good news about church.

The Fullness of the Good News of Easter

Easter is resurrection. Resurrection, of course, means that Jesus rose from the dead with an immortal body and has everlasting life. This concept by itself is too staggering for our finite minds to absorb. However, if we permit the cross and resurrection to enter our perception as two great and wonderful *koans*, we may be able to penetrate more deeply into the fullness of the resurrection in our minds and hearts. Drawing understanding from leaps of intuition within a spiritual framework, we may realize that, once again, the good news is actually "good-er" than we first thought.

What then can be the fullness of the good news of Easter and resurrection? Eventually, the resurrection will be *you* with your resurrected body in a transformed universe. More than that, the entire universe will become your resurrected body. The implications are enormous, for the universe will also become Christ's resurrected body. You will now completely enfold, embrace, and compenetrate each other. In the very best sense of the word, you will completely possess and be possessed by each other. And the wonder of the resurrection is that it will not diminish your individual personalities. On the contrary, it will enhance your personal growth to its fullest potential. It will be the ultimate "you" experiencing ultimate intimacy with Christ.

Similarly, the entire universe will also become the resurrected body of every other person gifted with resurrection. Once again, you will completely enfold, embrace, and compenetrate each other. Once again, there will be no diminishing of your uniqueness; the result, instead, will be ultimate personhood and ultimate encounter. The ultimate "you" will experience ultimate intimacy with all others.

Indeed, what is the goal of all religion, mysticism, romance, and love? It is to possess the beloved, whether Christ or others, to such an extent that, paradoxically, you become the beloved. Yet you do not cease to exist so that the beloved can become you. What we have then are the four ultimate heart wishes (to love, to be loved, to share, to blossom out as individual and community) extended to the infinity of their meaning. The result is the fullness of life, the fullness of the Reign of God, and the fullness of the good news of Easter.

The Fullness of the Good News of Pentecost

And what of Pentecost? Pentecost, of course, means wind, tongues of fire, charism, and conversion. The church of Christ was born in a spectacular fashion on that first Pentecost. Jesus' followers and their first converts underwent a profound religious experience that completely changed their lives. The tangible presence of the Spirit filled their minds and hearts. They experienced a deep and abiding peace with God and with one another. Their conviction and enthusiasm were contagious. Mass conversions occurred. In an outpouring of generosity, people unselfishly shared their possessions with one another. The church started with an explosion of faith and love that was felt, in time, to the ends of the earth.

But Pentecost means so much more than that. It is not just an event from the past. Pentecost is a process—and a process that is still going on today. It is a process of being swept up into the inner life of God that gives each of us an unbelievable foretaste of what the Risen Christ has attained—*if* we can leave ourselves open to it. And this is what we name "church."

Church as a Process of Easter and Pentecost

Church is the Risen Christ active among the people of God in an Easter-Pentecost process. Church is Christ *among* us taking what he has attained and sharing it with us to an unbelievable extent. We are not just passive recipients, however, because Christ empowers us to bring Easter and Pentecost to others. This is the genesis of all ministry. Christ is *with* us empowering us to take what he has attained and make it happen in other people's lives. Concretely, we are empowered by our baptism, confirmation, Eucharist, matrimony, orders, vows, charisms—the list is endless. And so we have two prepositions in our description of church: church is the Risen Christ *among* and *with* the people of God doing Easter-Pentecost process.

This then is the core of the good news about church. An integral part of this naming of church is the attempt to articulate the fullness of life that is the Reign of God. Most people in the church still center their spiritual lives around interior spirituality, the traditional spirituality filled with great riches amassed over centuries. Others have now uncovered a great spiritual richness flowing from justice activity. A chasm seems to exist in between. How can we introduce people centered around interior spirituality to the implications of justice spiritual insights? How can we reinforce justice ministry with an even greater amount of traditional spiritual richness? It is hoped that the resurrection spirituality and vision unfolding in the Christian discovery process will help to bridge the gap.

Although every vision illumines, every vision is also limited. Each vision is just that—a vision. We would need an infinity of visions (each nuancing and being nuanced by all the others) to fully encompass the Ultimate Reality. Even so, we must offer people a vision. Look at people in church today. They are often like sheep without a shepherd, like people lost in the desert. One perishes in the desert without a vision or an ultimate goal. Without a vision, why run the race? Particularly in justice ministry, a mystical vision, which is too often missing, is vital to success. Some visions that are totally other-worldly can tempt us to sit still in this life and ignore the challenge of systemic violence. Another matter altogether, though, is a vision that carries with it the possibility of an unbelievable foretaste right now recalling the fullness of the good news of Easter and Pentecost. Mysticism is an ingredient of successful justice ministry.

The early Christians had this vision of church as an Easter-Pentecost process. It was a Spirit-led process, a "Way." Throughout the gospel of the Holy Spirit (*The Acts of the Apostles*) we find references to "the Way" or its equivalent (for example, Acts 9:2, 16:17, 18:26, 19:9, 19:23, 24:14, 24:22). The believers moved through different towns, cities, and countries, teaching, preaching, and carrying the Word. Union with Christ and others was not attained by a rigid insistence on uniformity of organization. The early Christians realized that the process was better served by a pluriformity of organizational structures dependent on the local circumstances. Organization was there to serve the process; the process of "the Way" did not serve a particular organization.

"The Way" Becomes Organization

In a few short years we enter into the third millennium—the beginning of the third thousand years—of Christianity. A prophetic mantle is falling on our generation whether we like it or not. Exodus generations are certainly not chosen because they are the holiest. They are simply chosen. Squirm as we might we cannot get out from under the prophetic mantle. Our destiny is to lay the foundation for the third millennium.

To understand the third millennium of Christianity, it is necessary to go back to our roots and observe the church's struggle to become truly catholic, meaning universal, unlimited, including all. In the beginning, the Easter-Pentecost process was carried out in a Jewish model. The church's proto-theology used the Hebrew Scriptures and a Semitic view of life as its foundation. Early on, however, Stephen and other followers of Jesus began to realize that Easter and Pentecost were such cosmic events that they could not be encompassed by any one culture—even the Mosaic culture of revelation. Reaction set in and Stephen was the first to be killed (the fate of many change-agents throughout history). But a consciousness once raised could not be suppressed. Stephen's friends fled, probably to Antioch, and continued the work. As a result, persons of Greco-Roman culture began to enter the infant church community.

Paul, a missioner open to the cosmic implications of Easter and Pentecost, built on what had already been started by the others. Ever so slowly the Easter-Pentecost process began to manifest itself not only in terms of a Semitic culture but also in terms of a Greco-Roman culture. Once again, reaction set in, particularly among the followers of James of Jerusalem.

The ensuing struggle is telescoped and neatly packaged by Luke in *The Acts of the Apostles*. It is necessary to read between the lines in Luke's account because Luke has a tendency to put the best possible face on events. The struggle was much more prolonged and complicated than Luke would have us believe. When the dust finally settled, however, the Gentiles were in the church to stay, and with them came a new model for doing Easter-Pentecost process.

The early Christians were so filled with the adventure of
a Risen Christ that they not only let the Gentiles into the
church, but they allowed them to create a new model. Over
the centuries Greek philosophy took hold as a basis for doing
theology and Roman notions of power took hold as a basis
for church organization. But there is an old Arab saying that
once the camel gets its nose into the tent, eventually the
whole camel gets inside and pushes everything else out. Eventually the Greco-Roman model took over. With Constantine's
Edict of Milan, a symbiotic relationship began with the
Roman Empire. Increasingly the church started to imitate
the empire in its use of vertical, patriarchal power. Over the
centuries, the Greco-Roman model became an empire
model. The Jewish model and other incipient models of the
New Testament disappeared. In short, the pluriformity of the
New Testament had been suppressed.

As the migratory tribes of Europe encountered Christianity, they were offered but one choice: a Greco-Roman
empire model for doing Easter-Pentecost process. Had the
pluriformity of New Testament revelation not been suppressed, a wide variety of models would have ensued: Slavic,
Germanic, Gallic, Hispanic, Scandinavian, Anglo, Hiber-
nian—the list is endless. By the year 700, the church would
have been truly catholic!

With the Age of Discovery, Europe became aware of the
vast varieties of cultures throughout the globe. Here indeed
was the matrix for a wide variety of models for doing Easter-
Pentecost process. Missionary attempts were made. Reaction
set in once again and the empire model suppressed all other
models. If the church was not truly catholic by 700, it definitely should have been so by 1700! *Uniformity* in all aspects
of church life (a characteristic of one model) became synonymous with *union* with Christ and others. Irony indeed.
Inculturation allowed the Greco-Roman model to come into
existence, but it, in turn, prevented further inculturation.

Vatican II calls for a church that is truly catholic, universal, unlimited, including all. At Vatican II, the church challenged itself to become a world church.[1] We might call such a global church a world model of church, which would, in actuality, be a wide variety of models for doing Easter-Pentecost process.

Shifts as "the Way" Became a Church of One Organization

As the church came out of the catacombs, it developed a symbiotic relationship with the Roman Empire, which was also a love-hate relationship. The empire could help Christianity or the empire could hinder Christianity. The church gradually became the established religion of the empire. But the "empire" model, in turn, gradually became the established organization of the church. In other words, as the church converted the empire, the empire "converted" the church. The church began to mimic the empire, especially in terms of power. And so the three characteristics of the empire model arose:

- —All power in the hands of a few;
- —Only those in power decide who gets into power;
- —In a time of tension, organization "efficiency" gets preference over membership.

Such Orwellian characteristics may well have been needed in a past age. We will let the church historians argue over that. But they are absolutely counterproductive today. Why? Because such mechanisms are created to keep people at an external level of faith appropriation. All of the present goals of mission and ministry—and, in a particular way, justice ministry—are dependent on people acting from the internal levels of faith appropriation. To sow the seeds of ministry (parish renewal, vocation awareness, basic Christian community, lay leadership, justice endeavors—the list is endless) upon a soil that is continually held at an external level of faith appropriation is to resign oneself to getting ten cents on the dollar for one's ministerial efforts. And we wonder why the sowers (those in ministry) burn out!

A second drawback of the developed church was the way in which its teaching was formed. The traditional coherence in the church's catechetical or theological message was a deductive one based on the theology of the Council of Trent. It sufficed for a pre-Vatican II era of the socialization level of faith appropriation. Even then it could at times be a cruel coherence, for any person or idea that did not fit into its rigid schema was declared "non-person" and "non-idea."

A new coherence is needed. Any new coherence must, of course, contain the traditional content *and* the progress that is continually taking place; over and above that, however, it must be an inductive coherence: one that follows the logical order of Christian search and encounter experiences.

The deductive coherence of yesteryear helped people to *know* Christianity well but it left much to be desired in helping people to actually *experience* their Christianity. An inductive coherence can, of course, contain great catechetical or theological content. Moreover, it also encourages Christian experience by following the logical order of Christian growth. Such a "living" coherence will engender even more motivation for ministry, especially justice ministry.

Criteria for Future Church

If justice ministry is to be successful, the church must change. In fact, if any of the many goals of mission and ministry facing the church today are to be achieved, there must be change. But merely striving for change at the church level will not succeed. Why? Because opposition to change has merely to raise a voice. It is not even necessary for such a voice to be convincing in dialogue. If mere perplexity results, the status quo perdures and the people of God in general and God's *anawim* (God's "nobodies") in particular are ill-served.

In a world model of church we begin with the people of God living life. Daily they bring the gospel to bear on life. But daily they also bring life to bear on the gospel. The gospel, of course, challenges how life is to be lived. But the daily experiences of life give fuller meaning to what the gospel is all about. If the gospel light shines only on one facet of the diamond called reality (as in the empire model), then the implications of gospel only reflect back in one way. If the gospel light shines on all the facets (cultures, life situations, and so forth) of world reality (as in the world model), then the gospel of Christ can be reflected in all its possible glory.

It is well for the local churches in the developed countries to be aware that the majority of church members no longer reside in these developed countries, but in those that are underdeveloped or in the throes of development. It is here in particular among God's *anawim* that the world model of church is in genesis. This raises a particular challenge for local churches in the developed countries, and particularly in the United States. As the prophetic mantel of an exodus generation falls on the church in the United States, does it attempt to squirm out from under it and opt for the status quo of the church? Or does the church in the United States commit itself to what is unfolding in so many places around the world as the model of world church is in genesis? Does it rise to a Spirit-filled challenge? Or does it risk becoming a theological-pastoral-spiritual backwater in future church?

In the world model of church, of course, a pluriformity of theologies and a pluriformity of organizational flow charts (of power) will be visible that call for mission from everywhere to everywhere. No one way of doing either theology or organization will be perfect. Each local church must challenge and be challenged by every other local church. Hence, universal mission flows from everywhere to everywhere.

Today universal mission is beginning to result in a great cross-fertilization with particular insights coming from particular areas of the world.

1. Africa—As the seed of the gospel falls into the wide variety of African cultures, it begins to arise with the characteristics of each particular culture. The furthering of this process is called inculturation. Much more than mere cosmetic adaptation is involved here. Africa offers enormous potential for unfolding the full implications of what Christianity is all about.

2. Asia—Here is seen a mission of presence but it is an active presence centering around the primal cry for more, the primal religious experience, and the primal cry for help. The mission of presence requires dialogue with the other great religions of the world.

3. Latin America—There is a working out of what happens both in individuals and in systems when the poor cry out to Christ the Liberator.

4. Europe—Salvation history explores the ongoing implications of a God who walks with us through space and time. It extends from our earliest traditions to the most modern implications.

5. North America—To a greater and greater degree, North America is being called upon to deal with the implications of power. The theological and pastoral consequences of the many uses and abuses of power are to be explored. This effort must include all the systems in which life is lived (political, economic, social and ecclesiastical).

This, then, is the ultimate purpose of church: not to further its own institutional strength in a triumphal church, but to further the coming of the Kingdom in all aspects of life— religious, of course, but also political, economic, and social. The task is to help people and systems reflect the Reign of God.

The Commitment to not only Political, Economic and Social Justice but also to Religious Justice

More and more it is becoming obvious that the magnificent teachings of a church organization concerning political, economic, and social justice will go a-wasting unless there is a corresponding effort to address religious or ecclesiastical injustice. Credibility is increasingly lost to all, those inside the church, those alienated from church, and those outside the church, by not putting into practice what we preach.

In justice ministry, some ministers, as they hear the cries of those oppressed by political, economic, and social unjust systems, are tempted to ignore the fourth system, the ecclesiastical component. "Let's not dissipate our energies. Let's not get involved (although fully justified to do so) with in-house matters. Let's 'bite the bullet' so that we can serve the victims of political, economic, and social injustice."

This is a mis-reading of the signs of the times. If ecclesiastical injustice is ignored, a number of the present mechanisms of church structure stay in place. These mechanisms are geared to keep people at the socialization level of faith appropriation. We have seen that people at this level have a psychological bias against evaluating any political, economic, social, or religious system. Therefore, they cannot hear (or respond to) the challenge of church teaching on political, economic, or social systemic injustice. If the fourth component of justice (religious) is not practiced, the other three are doomed to failure.

If we work back through some of the signs of the times to the church we know, we can better understand the importance of ecclesiastical justice. Let's consider the children in Guatemala, half of whom never celebrate their eighth birthday. Why? Because they are already dead. These children are very susceptible to diseases such as gasteroenteritis because they suffer from chronic malnutrition. Their parents cannot earn a living wage to supply the basic family needs because the economic system, and often the land, is controlled by a wealthy minority and/or the military.

A North American Christian returns from Guatemala and tries to explain to other Christians that this situation continues because of policies of the United States government or various multinational corporations. The Christian urges others in the church community to challenge the multinationals and the making of foreign policy. A few Christians who have made an internal appropriation of their faith may hear this message. The largest number of Christians, the "cultural Christians" with an externally acquired faith, will most likely not respond. As discussed above, changing structures is beyond their faith level. Unfortunately, church structures as they are formed and operate today seem geared to keep believers at this third level of faith appropriation. Believers will contribute relief money, but not address the source of the problem—the international economic situation. People are reluctant to change their approach from symptom to system. What worked well in the past should work equally well today. Unfortunately, in most cases, Christians have not recognized that the world has changed. The world of crises today demands an exodus generation of Christians who are willing to look more closely at the signs of the times and at the church as "the Way." The component of justice must be practiced within the structure of church as well as without it. There is a direct causal relationship between religious justice and responding to the cries of God's "nobodies" throughout the world!

In evaluating our ministry today, we must ask ourselves if we are engaged in maintenance ministry or in transformation ministry. We can consider maintenance ministry only if what we are maintaining truly reflects and promotes the inbreaking of the Reign of God. If not, we need to turn to transformation ministry that will prepare and support believers eager to work toward the Reign of God.

And what will help us face the challenge of transformation ministry? It is hoped that many of the themes already explored in this book will be of assistance. But more is needed. Let us now turn to the "Great Coming Together" of Christianity: the Eucharist.

CHAPTER 7

━◆━◇━◆━◇━◆━◇━◆━◇━◆━

The Eucharist: "The Great Coming Together"

WITHIN THE COMMUNITY of Christ that is the church we find union with God and solidarity with all of God's peoples. The sacramental life of this church, through the Eucharist, provides strength for us to make lasting differences in the struggle for justice and peace. The power of the Eucharist is revealed by these words of Father Vincent Donovan:

> If any one sacrament stands for the whole of Christianity and the church, it is the Eucharist. It is the one sacrament that symbolizes fully what the Christian message is, what it means for the world. ... It is the presence of God in the world. It is the cross and the resurrection of Christ. It is the forgiveness of sins and reconciliation. It is salvation and the new creation. It is inexhaustible. It is Shalom. It is the breakthrough in the spiritualization of the material world.[1]

What is it that happens at the Mass event? We have to keep two things in mind. First, the Eucharist is a *cosmic* event that our finite minds and finite hearts are never going to fully encompass. Second, the key to understanding the Mass event is, of course, the Risen Christ who comes to us, the Word that was made flesh and dwells among us. We are now faced with two questions:

What is it that Christ does at the Mass event?
What is it that Christ enables us to do at the Mass
    event?

With these two questions in mind, let us consider the pastoral problem of explaining the Mass to a non-Christian who has never been to Mass.

In Japan, on occasion, a non-Christian would begin to stop by the mission. The Japanese would be interested or curious but still definitely on the fringe. One of the Christians would take this person under his or her wing and become a friend. It often happened that the friend would later announce that the non-Christian was considering attending Mass the following Sunday. Some sort of explanation of the Mass was in order. Explaining an event so theologically and spiritually complex to someone from a completely different linguistic and cultural background is an enormous pastoral challenge. How to get to the heart of the matter? Practically all of the usual pastoral tools are ineffective. All the usual approaches and explanations simply will not work with a Japanese non-Christian making a first inquiry. Theological terms, catechetical information, and pious urgings fall away, and one stands pastorally naked. Facing this non-Christian, one is also faced with one's self. Perhaps for the first time—and without recourse to the usual jargon—one must ask and answer the question: What is it that happens at the Eucharist? And so we come to four "movements" in the Eucharistic event:

- We speak to God.
- God speaks to us.
- We give to God.
- God gives to us.

That is really all that can be said in the first explanation; at a later session, we can extend the explanation:

- We speak to God as community (Introductory Rite).
- God speaks to us through Scripture (Liturgy of the Word).
- We give ourselves to God (Eucharistic Prayer).
- God gives of Self to us (Communion Rite).

With this stark, essential outline before us we can now begin to address our two earlier questions:

What is it that Christ does during the Mass event?
What is it that Christ enables us to do during the Mass
   event?

We Speak to God as Community

In the Eucharist, Christ is particularly operative as the Encounter Causer. We are not community just because we agree on a time and place to assemble, or because we agree on ceremonial procedures. No, it is Christ as the Encounter Causer who welds us into community. Thanks to Christ, there is the real possibility of loving beyond our own ability to love. There is the possibility of being loveable and attractive to others beyond our own ability. As we assemble in community, we bring with us our basic heart wishes, our religious longings, and our primal cries for help. Not only those of the immediate community but also those of the wider community — the world at large — are brought together and presented to God.

God Speaks to Us through Scripture

The Scripture passages are now no mere "lessons" to be taught, nor are they mere abstract moral urgings to be good. Rather, Christ makes Scripture come alive for us as encounter causer. The longings, hopes, and cries we bring to the first "movement" of the Mass as we speak to God meet "corresponding experiences" in Scripture. The Mass becomes the joiner, the facilitator.

$$\left.\begin{array}{l}\text{the experiences of the}\\\text{immediate community and}\\\text{those of the larger world}\end{array}\right\}\ \text{Mass}\ \left\{\begin{array}{l}\text{experiences in}\\\text{Scripture}\end{array}\right.$$

We must keep in mind that when using Scripture as encounter causer, the time-delay effect is operative. The actual encounter experiences may well take place a long time after the Mass itself is finished. Never limit the time of the Mass event to the time of the Mass ceremony.

We Give Ourselves to God

Bread and wine are brought forth as symbols of our daily lives and of the daily lives of all people on the face of the earth. So far, the bread and wine are mere human symbols somewhat analogous to thirteen stripes and fifty stars comprising a flag and signifying a nation. However, wonder of wonders, thanks to the Risen Christ, the symbols of our lives and the lives of all people become the Risen Christ's body and blood. What has happened? The Risen Christ has come among us with the inbreaking of the Reign of God. In the words of John Paul II:

> The goods of this world and the work of our hands — the bread and wine — serve for the coming of the *definitive Kingdom*, since the Lord, through his Spirit, takes them up into himself in order to offer himself to the Father and to offer us with himself in the renewal of his one Sacrifice, which anticipates God's Kingdom and proclaims its final coming.
> Thus the Lord *unites us with himself* through the Eucharist — Sacrament and Sacrifice — and he *unites us with himself and with one another* by a bond stronger than any natural union; and thus united, *he sends us* into the whole world to bear witness, through faith and works, to God's love, preparing the coming of his Kingdom and anticipating it . . . (*SRS*, 48).

Once again, the good news is "good-er" than we can imagine. Once again, we have to be willing to have the courage to think new thoughts and to be open to new experiences. We now have the potential not only to experience the presence of the Risen Christ but also to encounter union beyond imagining. For we are participating in the Eucharist as the "Great Coming Together."

In order to appreciate the potential before us, we must first attempt to free ourselves from the prison in which we exist. For the most part we are not even aware that we live in a prison called space-time. Because it marks the only existence we have ever had, it bothers us not at all. Yet our existence is very limited indeed. We receive our existence one second at a time, one tick of the clock at a time. The second ticked off is gone forever. The second to come is future. Similarly, in space our existence comes one "dot" at a time. If we are here, we cannot be there, or there, or over there. For people programmed for infinity by our Creator, this is a meager existence indeed. Even more troubling, the limitation goes beyond time and geography; it also applies to encounter and union in love with others. Such a meager existence hinders us, who are programmed for infinite love, from experiencing the full potential of love encounter.

Christ, however, provides the solution. Christ has gone through the evolutionary transition of death-unto-resurrection. Resurrection does not mean that Christ has gone out "there," out of space and time. It means rather that all of space and all of time are here and now to Christ, and that because of Christ we can have an analogous experience. Christ who is trans-temporal, trans-geographical, trans-cultural, and trans-social now gives us a share in his triumph.

Christ takes his life of two thousand years ago and melds it to our lives today. Christ plunges into our reality and says to us, "What are your basic heart wishes? They are now mine. Together we will strive to attain them. What are your sorrows, your hurts, your disappointments? Give me half. You are no longer alone. Anything you experience, no matter how commonplace, I find it an adventure to experience it with you."

We now plunge into Christ's life. What does that mean? It means that the gospels now become our biography—an integral part of our life. How can we make them come alive? Read the gospels in the first person. Everywhere it says "Jesus," "he," "him," or "his" insert your own name and "I," "me," or "my." See if you don't get a greater insight into what it means to be "in Christ," as St. Paul so often states. More important, experience the gospels coming alive as encounter causers.

Christ now takes our lives and the lives of those in need of justice and melds them together. No longer can I say that these injustices are happening only to my sisters and brothers around the world; they are happening to *me*! This is no mere theological poetic license; this is reality. The Risen Christ empowers us to experience a true compenetration of lives. Christ's question to Paul on the road to Damascus becomes our question: "Why are you persecuting me?" The Eucharist, the "Great Coming Together," challenges us to make those who suffer systemic injustice an integral part of our own personal spiritual lives, and an integral part of our various communities' spiritual lives (parish, school, religious community, diocese, and so forth). To do less is not to tap the fullness of the Eucharist. In the words of John Paul II:

> All of us who take part in the Eucharist are called to discover, through this sacrament, the profound *meaning* of our actions in the world in favor of development and peace; and to receive from it the strength to commit ourselves ever more generously, following the example of Christ, who in this sacrament lays down his life for his friends (cf. Jn. 15:13). Our personal commitment, like Christ's and in union with his, will not be in vain but certainly fruitful (*SRS*, 48).

All of this is now placed in the hands of God—an infinite act of love. Our lives melded together certainly do not amount to an infinite act of love, but our lives melded to Christ's life become an infinite act of love.

God Gives of Self to Us

People experience the Mass with a past-present orientation. Whether able to articulate it or not, most people sense that somehow the barrier between present and past is overcome. What Christ said and did for us in the past becomes here and now. The Mass is called memorial, but not in the sense that we just remember past events as on the Fourth of July; rather, the barrier between past and present is broken.

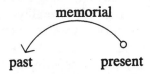

We must also learn to experience the Mass as future. Once again, thanks to the Risen Christ, the barrier between the present and future is somehow overcome. We should experience the Mass not only as memorial, but also as prophetic foretaste of the ultimate future.

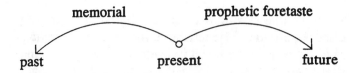

And so in the communion rite, Christ gives self to us, and, if we are open to it, Christ brings with himself an unbelievable prophetic foretaste of the ultimate reality: the fullness of life that lies in the Reign of God. Recall the fullness of the good news of Easter:

- the mutual enfolding, embracing, and compenetration of you and Christ,

- your ultimate personal growth,
- the ultimate you experiencing ultimate intimacy with Christ,
- the mutual enfolding, embracing, and compenetration of you and others,
- the ultimate you experiencing ultimate intimacy with others.

We can experience a prophetic foretaste of all this, beyond the wildest imagination, if we are open to its possibilities: love encounter with Christ, love encounter with others, and, in a special way, the possibility of love encounter with those in need of justice ministry. From the mystical depths of the Eucharist flows justice ministry!

You may well not experience much of this during the actual time of the Eucharistic ceremony. Once again, the time delay effect is in operation. Hours, days, or weeks may pass before actual encounters take place. Just be open. It's between your spirit and the Spirit of the Risen Christ as to when it happens.

Jesus at the Last Supper

Gathered with his friends, he hears the footsteps. He knows they are coming to get him. It will be soon — too soon — for his ministry is just getting under way.

Yet he could see it coming. It all went back to that decision — to that love commitment that he made. Baptized by John he crossed the Jordan valley and, led by the Spirit, he climbed the hills into a deserted and desert area where he literally and figuratively sweated it out. He was all too conscious of his vast abilities and found himself at a fork on the way of life. Marshalling his talents and going for power would be easy. The local political situation was tranquil under Roman occupation, yet the tranquility was only apparent. It would be easy to bring it all tumbling down. In the vacuum created by chaos, it would be easy to move in. A shady deal here, a double-cross there, it would not take long. No necessity to listen to the masses, just quickly set up a new pyramid of power to replace the former pyramid. Then act quickly before Rome could mobilize, and duplicate the process over the horizon. Once started, it would be hard to stop—the whole Mediterranean basin beckoned. And after that—well, time enough for that later. . . .

The gospels present the temptation of Jesus in rather antiseptic terms. Beneath those stolid words lies real temptation, especially the temptation to the lust for power.

Or—does Jesus follow his heart, continuing on the intimacy-action spiral and responding to the call to the fullness of life for himself and for all creation? So he opts for the inbreaking of the Reign of God and begins his journey. It is a ministerial journey that first concentrates in Galilee. He is watched, he is harassed but the ministry goes on. Finally he heads for Jerusalem where all the systems are ultimately answerable to the Roman system. The implications of the impending Reign of God now begin to heat up. There is the call not only to personal holiness but also to systemic holiness. Events speed up. And now Jesus hears the footsteps.

No defeatist, Jesus is not a person of violence, but neither will he tolerate the triumph of violence. As the intimacy-action spiral begins to reach its climax, he arrives at the intuitive moment: "My friends, we may be defeated in the here and now, but the Reign of God will triumph." He reaches out beyond the immediate limitations of that place and that moment and begins to embrace all space and all time. So begins the Eucharistic event.

The Eucharist then is the "Great Coming Together": the union of divine and human life, the union of all human life as one. As Jesus begins his sacrifice, we realize that our self-offering is a participation in Christ's self-offering. All of life comes to bear on the Eucharist; the Eucharist comes to bear on all life:

life ⟶ Mass ⟶ life

All of life—happenings and non-happenings; joys, sorrows, hopes, longings; of individual, of immediate community, of world-wide community—are to come flowing into the Mass. More creative thought needs to be given to the first "movement" (Introductory Rite) to make this happen. If we are not carefully prepared to speak to God, the Introductory Rite is reduced to a mere liturgical warmup exercise. If that happens, there is danger of all of life not flowing into the Mass. Then why are we at Mass, except perhaps to get away from life for a moment? The more life flows into the Eucharist, the more the Eucharist will then empower us to do life. The more the cries of God's *anawim* (the powerless, the marginated) flow into the Eucharistic action, the more people will be empowered to respond.

There is a great irony in all of this. The Eucharistic event, which is to be the great "sign" of life, is in danger of becoming something of a "counter-sign." The present system so limits the number of ministers of the Eucharistic action that the people of God are being short-changed. Already there are close to two thousand priestless communities in the United States and close to 160,000 priestless communities in the world. Future projections are even more abysmal. Stop-gap measures are exactly that, and provide no lasting solution. Tragedy indeed.

Eucharist and Justice

The church proclaims that justice is an integral part of evangelization. But there is danger of it remaining just that— a proclamation. Proclamation becomes commitment only when people "own" the teaching at an experiential level. That is the purpose of all the stages of Christian discovery. The process culminates in the Eucharistic action, the "Great Coming Together." Here our lives and the lives of those in need of justice ministry come together. From the intimacy of the Eucharistic event flows justice action.

It is well to bear in mind the roots of the Mass:

Exodus ———→ Passover ———→ Last Supper ———→ Mass

The exodus was no mere religious procession. It was a political, economic, social, and religious event. The Jews found themselves immersed in unjust systems and decided it was impossible for them to remain under Egyptian oppression. Under the guidance of God as Liberator they took action. We must be careful not to relegate the exodus to the level of one more biblical story. It is one of the great themes that runs not only through the Hebrew Scriptures but through the New Testament as well.

The chosen people never lost sight of the exodus. Through centuries of oppression they have kept living contact with the exodus through the instrumentality of Passover. When Jesus heard the footsteps of systemic injustice guided by the Roman Empire, he gathered in Passover for the Last Supper. It is *last* but it is also *first*. For now begins the "Great Coming Together." The Mass then is the heir of great tradition and, hence, of great challenge. Only if we are aware of the great political, economic, social, and religious roots of the Mass will it be the "Great Coming Together."

The Eucharist, like the other sacraments, is not an isolated reality, serving as a mere end in itself. The Eucharist empowers people for ministry, for community building, for the inbreaking of the Reign of God. It calls our attention to the fact that all life experiences are holy and points out the sacramentality of all of human life. Within the Eucharist, then, lies the beginning of solidarity.

> *Solidarity* helps us to see the "other" — whether a *person, people or nation* — not just as some kind of instrument, with a work capacity and physical strength to be

exploited at low cost and then discarded when no longer useful, but as our "neighbor," a "helper" (cf. Gen. 2:18-20), to be made a sharer, on a par with ourselves, in the banquet of life to which all are equally invited by God (*SRS*, 39).

In *Sollicitudo Rei Socialis* John Paul II continues by discussing how solidarity can lead to peace and to authentic development that will "anticipate" the glory of the Reign of God. The encyclical emphasizes the need to establish solidarity in taking on the "structures of sin" that are obstacles to peace and human dignity.

Chapter 8

Understanding
the "Structures of Sin"

OUR COMPREHENSION of gospel values flowing from the Eucharist as the "Great Coming Together" of God and God's people moves us to apply these values to real situations in solidarity with all of God's peoples. This is an essential task of the Christian community. In *Sollicitudo Rei Socialis* John Paul II describes Christian solidarity as:

> . . . *a firm and persevering determination* to commit oneself to the *common good*; that is to say to the good of all and of each individual, because we are *all* really responsible *for all*. This determination is based on the *solid* conviction that what is hindering full development is that desire for profit and that thirst for power already mentioned. These attitudes and "structures of sin" are only conquered — presupposing the help of divine grace — by a *diametrically opposed attitude*: a commitment to the good of one's neighbor with the readiness, in the gospel sense, to "lose oneself" for the sake of the other instead of exploiting him, and to "serve him" instead of oppressing him for one's own advantage [cf. Mt. 10:40-42; 20:25; Mk. 10:42-45; Lk. 22:25-27] (*SRS*, 38).

As pastoral ministers, we know what our task is: to help sisters and brothers and the systems in which we live reflect the Reign of God. The tools we have examined so far — the missing stones in the arch of integral justice — help us to understand how Christian faith develops through personal encounter with Scripture, with Christ, and with the church of Easter-Pentecost process. One missing stone remains, however, and that stone is vital to completion of the arch. Christians ready to commit themselves to justice ministry must understand the relationship between the systems in which they live and the values that give birth to those systems, in short, what comprises "structures of sin."

If someone were to go through a city and shoot a number of children, everyone would be immediately enraged by this Herod-like act. However, in the slums of some of the great cities of the world (or in countries such as Guatemala, as was previously mentioned), 50 percent of the children die before their eighth birthday, but little outrage is generated. Why is it that these deaths do not outrage us in the same way? As "members one of another" we must learn to evaluate the systems that create conditions of hunger, poverty, illiteracy, war, refugees, violation of human rights, and environmental destruction. We must begin by looking very carefully at these sinful structures that have become the systems in which we live, the systems we commonly depend upon, and the systems that direct our lives.

People Change Structures . . .

Imagine yourself in space for a number of centuries. Your main occupation has not been "out there," however, but "down here." You have been closely observing the unfolding of human structures on the face of the global village called Earth. As organizations become more complex, there is a need for a division of labor, and specialized groups are formed. Some people are called upon to make and enforce laws, some are called to defend, some are called to manage economic structures, some are called to guide the day-to-day living in social structures, some are called to nourish the religious aspirations of the people—the list is endless.

So far, so good. Now comes the sad part. The self-interest of many specialized groups begins to get out of hand. The specialized groups now want more advantages and power than they require. Within each group the self-interest of the group itself becomes more important than the common good of the whole people. This is lamentable but readily understandable. Humans tend to be selfish, to grab a bigger piece of the pie than they need or deserve. This is the human condition.

So far, so human. Now comes the dangerous part. In order to continue its control of an oversized piece of the power, the group sets up its organization in such a way that those in power decide who gets into power. The group now begins to perpetuate its hold on the overextended power and prerogatives it has attained.

. . . Structures Change People . . .

Now comes the truly insidious part. In order to prevent any challenge to its continual and overextended control, the group begins a massive educational effort. Through this propaganda, the self-interest of the group gradually becomes identified with the common good of the whole. Now if one challenges a political policy, one is unpatriotic. If one questions a military budget, one is a dupe of the enemy. If one investigates a social structure, one is tearing the fabric of society. If one challenges the use of religious power, one is irreligious, and so forth. Who wants to be unpatriotic, disloyal, antisocial, or irreligious? The law of moral entropy sets in. Gradually, the status quo is accepted by all; even worse, not only is it accepted by all, it becomes an integral part of their worldview. The structures themselves are so ingrained that even those who suffer from the mal-distribution of power will now resist change. In this way, even the victim becomes part of the problem. A relationship of dependency and powerlessness is not only legalized but canonized.

. . . People Change Structures

Fortunately, not only the law of moral entropy but also the Spirit hovers over the surface of Earth. Gradually, some people begin to see the flaws in all of this. In the beginning it is a tiny minority lacking power and influence. The farther out on the margin one is, the easier it is to spot the flaws: for example, a black woman in the "colored" section at the back of the bus in Montgomery, Alabama; someone living in the slums; or someone living in a developing or underdeveloped country. In the past, unfortunately, these voices were often snuffed out. It was easy for the specialized groups to seize the legal and moral high ground to defame these voices in the wilderness, to isolate them, and eventually to smother their cries.

In recent times, however, a new phenomenon is taking place. The causes, of course, are manifold, but we will focus on merely one. With the advent of instantaneous communication, ideas, events, theological insights, and raised consciousness can travel the world unbelievably fast. A remarkable co-worker of the Spirit has come into being. The prophetic insights of the few now have the potential to become the viewpoint of the many. It goes without saying that instantaneous communication by itself will accomplish nothing. The nervous system of the human body carries out its magnificent task of transferring messages back and forth only if the body possesses life. Likewise, instantaneous communication needs the Spirit of Christ, the liberating effect of the gospel, and much ministerial endeavor to carry out its analogous task of rendering the world as one body.

The cries of the marginated can now be heard in a way not thought possible a few decades ago. Even the silence of the smothered cries can now be heard! Witness the four American women missioners killed in El Salvador in 1980 and, through them, the cries of more than 70,000 anonymous victims. Try as General Jaruzelski did, he could not suppress Solidarity—not only because it was so strong in Poland, but also because it was so strongly supported outside Poland. Networking on a global scale is now possible. Global communications working with the Spirit can now uncover and name layer upon layer of biases against groups of people, and the myths that have been borne in these biases. Unjust structures of all types — political, economic, social and, sad to say, religious — now face a formidable challenge.

After working with the major religious superiors of Australia and before beginning a series of workshops on ministry in that country, I was interviewed on a television program. At the end of the program, my interviewer requested a one-sentence summary of the implications for future ministry. "There are no strangers in the world, only brothers and sisters," was my reply.

The Relationship between People and Structures

Let us now "exegete" the above reflection.

A small group seizes much power. This is an all too common fact. Lust for power seems to be the greatest addiction on the face of the earth. This is not the case of an individual or group seeking to be empowered, but rather it is the seizing of power over and above what is necessary for the common good, and a seizure of power that undermines the common good.

Not only is power seized, but a plan arises to perpetuate the control of power. This is done by changing structures so that only those in power decide who gets into power. Those in control decide who gets into the inner circle and begin to perpetuate themselves. As a result, the structures are changed or deformed. *What began as personal sin now becomes systemic or structural sin.* The system itself becomes both addicted and addicting.

Power is protected not only by revamped structures but also by myth. "Myth" is used not in the sense of fable, but as a powerful story or value or tradition with its own symbols that give meaning and identity to people. Generally, myths have a good core value and show life as it should be. Myths, however, lend themselves easily to twisted interpretations. An example may help. Loyalty to a country is valued by most of its citizens. The defense budget of this country is projected at three hundred billion dollars for the coming year. A citizen questions this allocation to defense. Other citizens interpret any questioning of the defense allocation not as a matter of fiscal responsibility but as a lack of patriotism. The good core value of the myth (loyalty to one's country) has now taken on a twisted interpretation (support of an unquestioned defense budget is essential for loyalty to one's country).

Twisted interpretations of myths often present the self-interest of a small power group as being identical with the common good. While the high defense allocation may benefit a small group of industrialists, is it in the best interests of the common good? Could part of the money be better spent on health, housing, or education? Does the lack of allocation to health, housing, and education actually perpetuate the power of the small power group? Has the twisted interpretation become a part of the myth itself? The myth's twisted interpretation may have become so powerful that even citizens who might wonder why more money is not spent in areas other than defense take no actual action for change. Citizens may have become so loyal to the twisted myth that, in fact, they protect the very systems that are harming them. It should be obvious that similar analogies could be made of other systems, whether they be social, economic, political, or religious. Myths with good core values, *and* their twisted interpretations, underlie all of these systems.

In the past, prophetic voices often cried out. Myths, with their twisted interpretations, were invoked to counter these prophets' voices. Before a prophetic voice could spread far, it was silenced. Generations, perhaps centuries, later the true import of the prophetic voice was recognized but its contemporaneous impact was lost. Silence reigned and so did the unjust structures.

Today, however, a new factor has entered the human equation. Instantaneous communication, coupled with the fact that millions of people have moved beyond the socialized level of faith appropriation, makes possible a quantum leap in the human condition. We are an exodus generation and we do live in a time of great hope. In *Sollicitudo Rei Socialis* John Paul II noted that this eve of the third Christian millennium is characterized by "widespread expectancy, rather like a new 'Advent' " (*SRS*, 4). Our time does have new prophets; as we listen to their voices today, what insights do we get?

The Primary Villain — Flawed Systems

Human life is lived within political, economic, social, and religious systems. In many instances there is a vertical interpretation of life. Power is crucial. Those with power dominate; the rest are forced to submit. Often it is an oligarchy that holds a monopoly on power. Individuals either submit in order to maintain a minimal self-image, a sense of belonging and survival, or, failing to submit, they are branded as non-persons.

In this vertical interpretation of life where power flows only from the top, unjust systems are constructed *and* protected. Myths, which may have good values at their core, are given a twisted interpretation to favor the system. As time passes, the myth and its twisted interpretation become synonymous.

Imagine the following scenario. A slave whose family is suffering from malnutrition steals a chicken. On being caught, the slave is confronted by his master, the sheriff, and a member of the clergy. The master recounts the sacrifices he personally has made to keep the plantation a success for the benefit of all, including the slaves. How could the slave go against the good order of the plantation? The sheriff informs the slave that he has broken the law. How could he commit a crime? The clergyman declares that a commandment of God has been violated. How could he commit a sin? The slave has no answer — as long as the others define the terms. The only answer for the slave is to rise above the terms imposed and ask the question: What is the real issue? The real issue, of course, is slavery—systemic injustice! The myths of good order and well-being are hopelessly confounded by the twisted interpretation introduced by the sinful system of slavery. But as long as the slave stays trapped within the terms set by the system, he cannot answer the questions of the owner, the sheriff, or the religious leader, except to admit that he is against good order, economic stability, or is antisocial or irreligious. Only by rising above the system is it possible to get to the real issue.

As in the scenario above, law is usually called upon to serve the system. The correct purpose of law is to serve the common good of the people within the system: to put checks and balances on the use of power lest it get out of control, and to safeguard the powerless. Law operates with power, but power is necessary even for a good system to work. Unfortunately, power is addictive—the most addictive of all addictions!

When called upon to serve an unjust system, the law, for the most part, ignores its two-fold purpose of providing checks and balances and of safeguarding the powerless. Instead, the group in power subverts and uses it to preserve the status quo, which is the mal-distribution of power within the system. But since it is the "Law," people are commanded to obey it; and because it is the "Law," they feel obliged to conform. Under the system, unjust laws and morality become synonymous. The system begins to take on a life of its own. Even individuals holding unjust power become secondary to the system itself; they can be replaced and yet the system perdures. As holders of power serve the unjust system in an unquestioning way, they exacerbate the problem. The system, of course, handsomely rewards those who serve it and viciously punishes these same people if they began to critique it. Like Dr. Frankenstein's monster, or the computer "Hal" in the movie "2001," or the Canaanite deity, Moloch (Lev.

18:21; Ezra 16:20 ff), the systems begin to take on a life of their own.

In a world of unjust systems, discernment becomes imperative. It is essential to determine who is holding unjust power, to challenge these persons, to alert functionaries who have allowed themselves to be co-opted by the system, and to empower victims who may previously have accepted the system in an unquestioning way. In the ideal system shown in Figure 1, in which the circles represent the core value of the myth and the myth's interpretation, the circles coincide. In this ideal world, morality and legality will always coincide, as will authority and power.

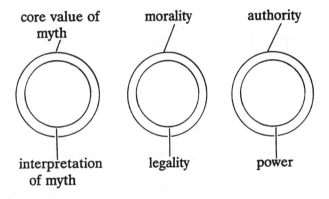

Just Systems

Fig. 1

In unjust systems, however, the circles move as seen in Figure 2. Parts of these moveable circles may well overlap and only in those circumstances (the shaded areas) does the system function in a just manner. On the other hand, discernment quickly shows that in many instances the circles do not overlap. The myth's twisted interpretation, which may have become part of the myth itself, undermines the myth's core value. What is legal may now be immoral. And, even worse, what is moral may have become illegal! Those in power, although possessing the symbols of authority, lack genuine authority. Paradoxically, those deprived of power (the power-less) may be empowered with great moral authority.

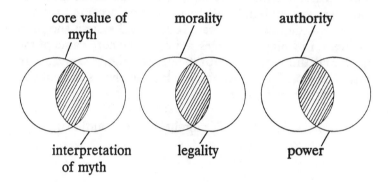

core value of myth / interpretation of myth

morality / legality

authority / power

Unjust Systems

Fig. 2

Who Is Your God?

There is a role for God even in unjust systems. Unjust systems regard God, the real God of infinite possibilities, as dangerous, and sometimes try to eliminate God. But history has shown this to be a difficult task. Far better to domesticate God, to contain and encapsulate God. An effective tactic for an institution is to create God in its own image and likeness or, actually, to create an *image* of God in its own image. This pre-fabricated God is not only non-threatening to the system, but can, in fact, be used by the system to maintain its dominance. "This is God's will," then, is invoked as a blessing to support an unjust system, and working "against God's will" becomes the ultimate sanction to be used against anyone who critiques the system.

A "Bifocal" God

Many such images of "God" exist, but two are particular favorites: the "bifocal" God and the "parade" God. The bifocal God wears bifocals, of course, and splits reality through the middle as shown in Figure 3.

spiritual	sacred	eternal
material	secular	temporal

Fig. 3

The upper level is all important and the lower level usually runs a distant second. If one's God is a bifocal God, then Jesus came to bring salvation, redemption, and liberation, almost exclusively in the upper level. Church is restricted to ministry activities in the upper level. Church may allow itself to participate in lower level activities to relieve the symptoms of injustice, but it is considered to be overstepping its bounds if it critiques the systems that cause the symptoms in the first place. (Conversely, in this bifocal view, the upper level is the exclusive domain of church and no life experiences in the lower level should be brought to bear on the theology and ministry of church.)

If a bifocal God is alive and well in a person's heart, then that person cannot hear the justice message of the church. Although we keep trying to introduce justice ministry in the church, effective programs of justice ministry will not be possible unless the need for justice is already perceived by the Christian through Scripture and Christ. That, in turn, is not possible unless the bifocals are taken off God at an early stage of the Christian discovery process.

A Holistic View of God

We need to rediscover the more holistic view of ministry and spirituality found in the New Testament, the daughter

of the Hebrew Scriptures. One of Christianity's great para-
doxes is that the New Testament, although written in Greek,
reflects, for the most part, a Semitic view of life, which was
holistic. For example, when Paul speaks to us of *flesh*, we
hear a correlation with the lower level of concerns in Figure
3. When he speaks of *spirit*, we sense a correlation with the
top level. That is what we have been conditioned to hear.
Actually, when Paul speaks of *flesh*, he is saying something
much closer to the following: "This is the total body-person
(upper and lower levels) who has opted not to encounter, not
to love, not to evolve toward the fullness of the Reign of
God." Conversely, when Paul speaks of *spirit*, he is saying:
"This is the total body-person who has opted to encounter,
to love, to evolve towards the fullness of the Reign of God
in all aspects of life."

In the New Testament, the material is not separated from
the spiritual, the secular is not totally separated from the
sacred, and the temporal has eternal overtones. Only a recov-
ery of the New Testament's holistic view of life will free us
from the dualistic viewpoint that limits our hearing of the
fullness of the good news about God, Christ, and church.

The "Parade" God

Another pre-fabricated image of God is a "parade" God
who insists that one remain at the parade or socialization
level of faith appropriation. Somehow, to move beyond this
level is to question God, or to become disloyal, over-critical,
or less holy. The worst thing that can happen to any unjust
system is to have a number of its members move beyond the
socialization level. Once members get well into an interior
appropriation of their faith, they begin to evaluate systems,
with the result that the maintenance of the status quo of the
unjust system is endangered.

The "Real" God

And who is the God we encounter through Scripture,
Christ, and church? It is a God who responds to the deepest

longings of our hearts and a God who is still actively involved in creation. Creation is not something that happened a long time ago; it is happening now, not in the sense that God continues to create from nothing, but in the sense that God has a continuing plan of development for all of creation. God wants us to complete the work that remains yet undone. In doing this work, God asks us "to act justly, to love tenderly, and to walk humbly" (Mic. 6:8) and to be "members one of another" (Rom. 12:5). This God is my personal God and yours and the God of all people, especially the downtrodden and the otherwise forgotten. This God, who is equally concerned with our entire being, both matters of spirit and of flesh, speaks to us through Scripture, through Christ, through church, and through union with others in words that comfort, support, and encourage. This is the "real" God who empowers us to work for a world transformed in accordance with God's plan.

Changing People Changing Structures

CHRISTIANS TODAY LIVE in a time of great stress and also a time of great hope. As pastoral ministers, we must work so that people enter in through church doors with a purpose—to encounter the Good News of the Reign of God, and so that they go out through the doors carrying with them the seeds of the Reign of God. Eager as we are to preach the Good News, to complete the stone arch of justice, or to get the justice ministry cart to the crest of the hill, we must be careful to listen to the questions people are asking—or are not asking. We must stimulate them to search for meaning in life and we must be prepared to search along with them. The great religions of the world are, at their core, attempts to address the mystery at the center of life itself. They have gained adherents and enriched people's lives because they offer people a way to deal with these cosmic concerns. Any religion must respond to the deepest longings of human hearts—to love, to be loved, to share, and to blossom.

Not all Christians with whom we have regular contact view religion in this way. Many, as we have said, are simply going through the motions because their parents were members of the church. It is important for pastoral ministers to learn to know and understand these people and their faith—to look at the soil of the justice message, to understand the nature of the soil, and to help it grow more fertile.

As pastoral ministers, we can help individuals express and satisfy their deepest longings by encountering God and other people through love. When Christian development occurs as a logical process with a logical order, the believer is led into

Scripture to encounter the Word of God in the Risen Christ, and then outward to encounter all of God's creation in love. Jesus came to free us *from* sin *for* encounter. Deliverance from sin is still immensely important, because sin is such an obstacle to love encounter with God and others.

Armed with a new spirituality that provides inward strength and outward direction, the believer is empowered to become part of a church that is a process rather than just an organization. The process of church unites all of God's world in a new "Way" and, in the Eucharist, brings all of this world before the same altar in love. United in love, the implications of Christianity deal not only with personal sin, the need for personal *metanoia* and the call to personal holiness; they must also deal with systemic sin, the need for systemic *metanoia* and the call to systemic holiness in all of the systems in which life is lived.

We must help individuals to understand that one person's lack of justice or peace today is everyone's problem and that activity on behalf of justice and peace is no longer an available option but an *urgent necessity*. Concern for a dying eight-year-old child in Guatemala must penetrate our hearts and minds in the same way it would if the child lived next door to us or was a member of our family. Christian concern for justice for all of God's people is part of the actual core of Christian life. The dying child in Guatemala is encompassed in our loving and being loved, in our blossoming, and in our sharing.

Pastoral ministers who understand these deep primal needs can lead others to satisfy their longings through encounters with God and others by means of Scripture, Christ, and church. As faith deepens and takes on not only a personal dimension but also a world dimension, people *will* change. These changing people will be empowered to change sinful structures. Reformed structures will, in turn, enrich the lives of all of God's peoples. This is integral justice — a probing concern for God's "nobodies" and a commitment for justice that flows from Christian faith, from Scripture, from Christ, and from church.

Notes

1. Barriers to Integral Justice

1. *The Road to Damascus: Kairos and Conversion* (Washington, D.C.: Center of Concern, 1989), p. 12.

2. Levels of Faith Appropriation

1. In analyzing the levels of faith appropriation I owe a large debt of gratitude to James Fowler's work on faith development. See especially Fowler's central book, *Stages of Faith: The Psychology of Human Development and the Quest for Meaning* (Harper & Row, 1981). As developed in *Integral Justice* the levels of faith appropriation view faith growth through the optic of the pastoral implications for successful justice ministry. The author takes full responsibility for the following interpretation. See also my *Evangelization and Justice* (Orbis, 1982) for an in-depth discussion of these stages.

2. Archbishop Oscar Romero, *Voice of the Voiceless* (Orbis, 1985), p. 83.

3. The Christian Discovery Process

1. The Christian discovery process is described in greater detail in two of my earlier books, *Evangelization and Justice* (Orbis, 1982) and *So You Want To Do Ministry* with James DiGiacomo (Sheed & Ward, 1986).

5. The New Spirituality

1. Donal Dorr, *Spirituality and Justice* (Orbis, 1984), p. 9.
2. Ibid., pp. 131-132.

6. Church as Easter-Pentecost Process

1. See Karl Rahner, "Towards a Fundamental Theological Interpretation of Vatican II," *Theological Studies* 40, no. 47 (December 1979).

7. Eucharist: "The Great Coming Together"

1. Vincent J. Donovan, *The Church in the Midst of Creation* (Orbis, 1989), pp. 75-76.